DREAMS OF WAKANDA

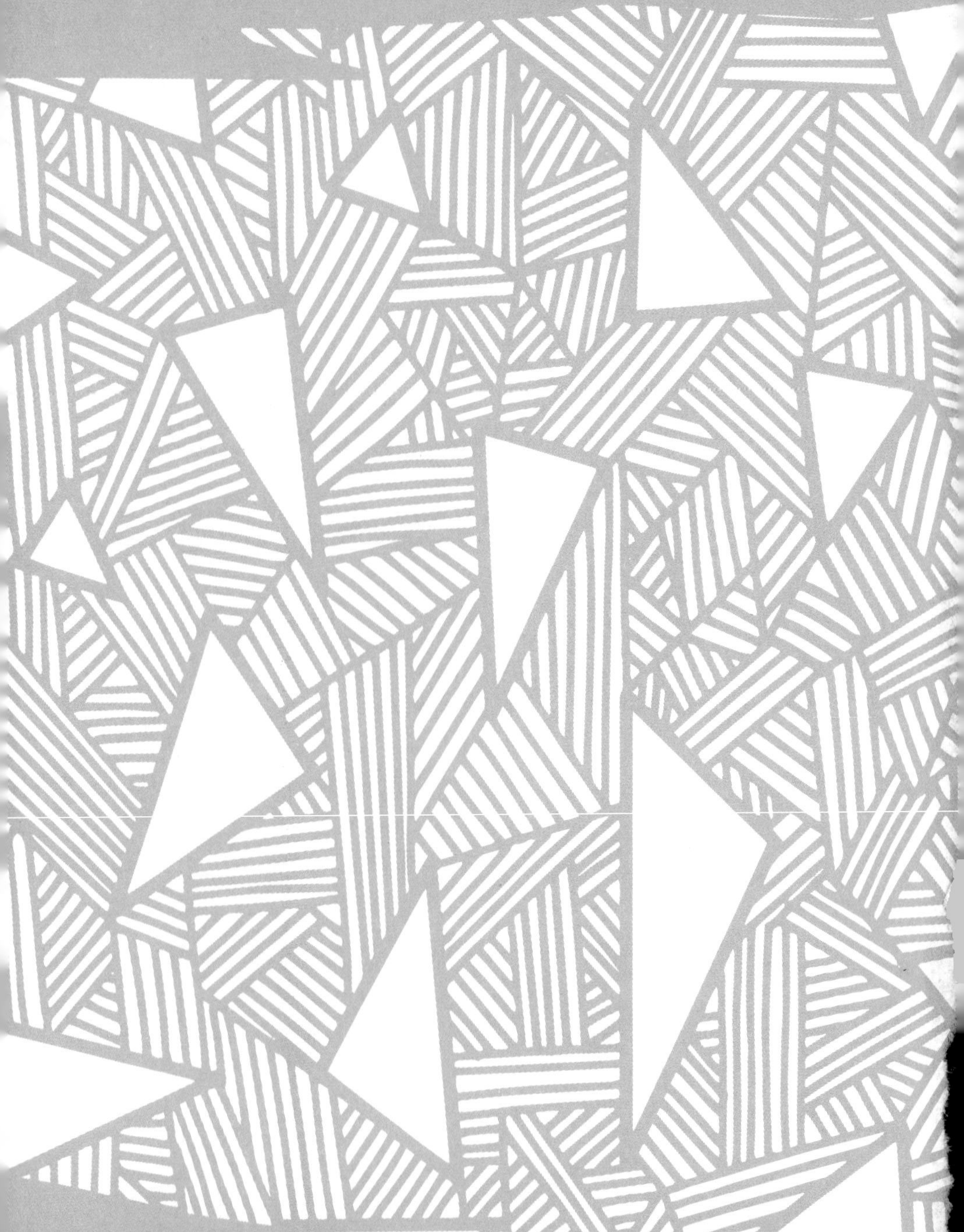

DREAMS OF WAKANDA

**CREATORS, WRITERS, AND COMICS LEGENDS ON
THE IMPACT OF MARVEL STUDIOS' *BLACK PANTHER***

NIC STONE ◆ YONA HARVEY ◆ AARON C. ALLEN

FREDERICK JOSEPH ◆ TRE JOHNSON

HANNAH GIORGIS ◆ GIL ROBERTSON IV

MARLENE ALLEN AHMED ◆ RUTH E. CARTER

DWAYNE WONG OMOWALE

SUYI DAVIES OKUNGBOWA ◆ ARVELL JONES

MAURICE BROADDUS

ILLUSTRATED BY MATEUS MANHANINI

NEW YORK

© 2022 MARVEL

All rights reserved.

Published in the United States by Del Rey,
an imprint of Random House, a division of
Penguin Random House LLC, New York.

DEL REY and the CIRCLE colophon are registered trademarks of
Penguin Random House LLC.

Hardback ISBN 978-1-9848-2617-6
Ebook ISBN 978-1-9848-2618-3

Interior and endpaper illustrations: Mateus Manhanini

Printed in the United States of America on acid-free paper

randomhousebooks.com

1st Printing

First Edition

Book design by Edwin Vazquez

We all know the truth: more connects us than separates us. But in times of crisis the wise build bridges, while the foolish build barriers. We must find a way to look after one another, as if we were one single tribe.

—T'CHALLA, *BLACK PANTHER*

CONTENTS

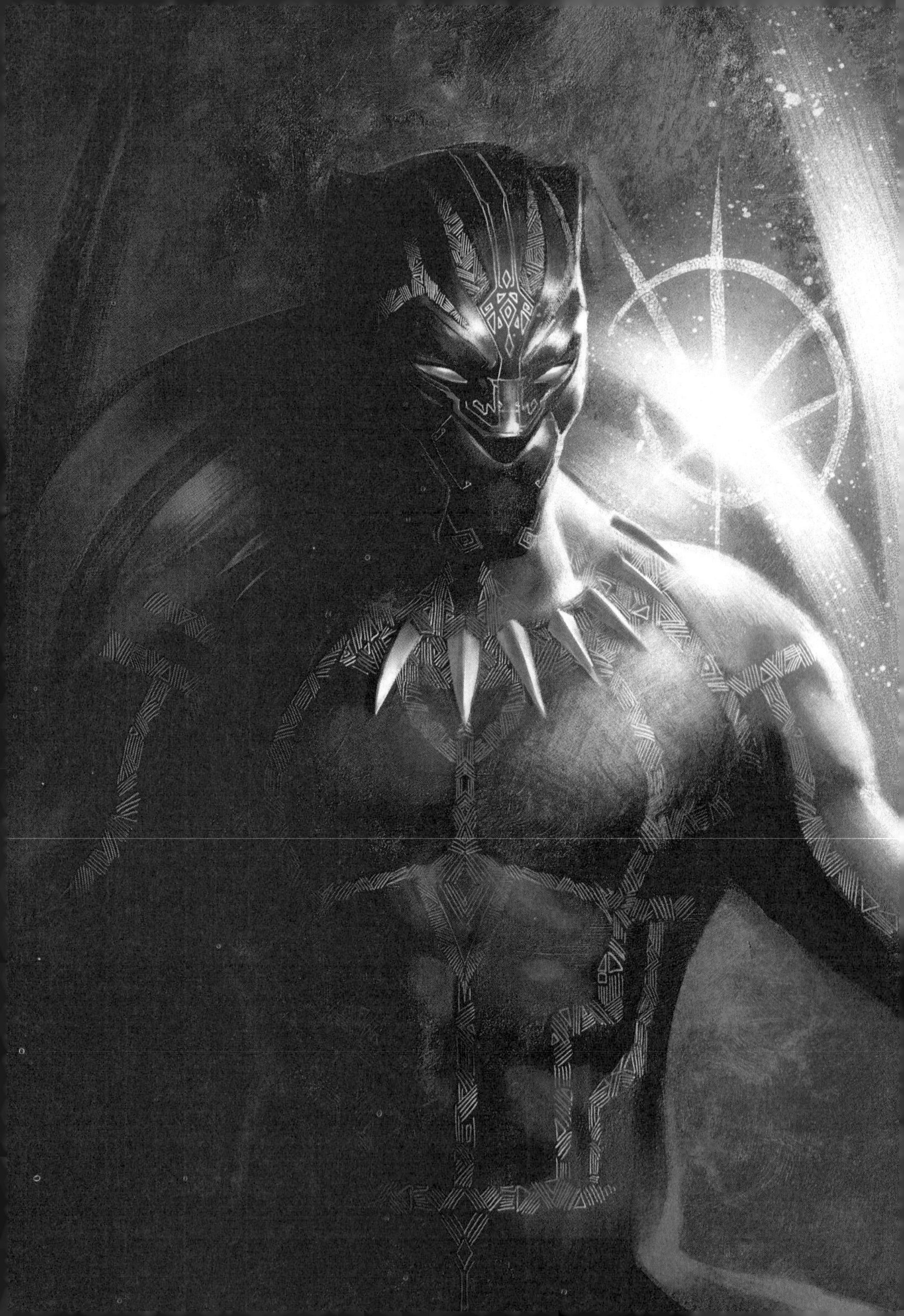

FOREWORD

Nic Stone

2016 WAS A WEIRD YEAR FOR ME. I'd sold my debut young-adult novel in 2015, but it wasn't scheduled to be published until 2017, and though I was working on new stuff, it was with great trepidation—I very deliberately wrote stories about Black kids, and at that point, they weren't exactly in high demand.

Honestly, prior to 2018, when the first Marvel Studios' *Black Panther* film was released, trepidation was a *thing* in the hearts of many Black people attempting to forge or maintain careers in storytelling and entertainment spaces—this *is* a book of essays about how said film impacted a variety of lives, and you *are* reading the foreword, after all.

As for *my* story: I'd been an avid reader as a child, but for reasons I couldn't articulate back then, the practice had lost its savor as I tumbled headlong into adolescence. It would be years before I'd figure out the root of my sudden disdain for books. Once I did, I realized that all of the ones I was told I *had* to read either had soundly awful depictions of Black people or no Black people at all.

We gravely underestimate the damage this does to the developing identities and worldviews of young people. And not just Black ones, either. In many ways, what we read in books and see and hear in popular culture informs the way we view—and therefore *treat*—other human beings. Ourselves included.

Yes, I'd decided not to believe the messages from those high-school books: I was not minimally intelligent (like Jim from *The Adventures of Huckleberry Finn*) nor destined to be a scapegoat (see Tom Robinson from *To Kill a Mockingbird*), and I wasn't powerless with regard to my own destiny (shout-out to Crooks from *Of Mice and Men*). But I was still utterly petrified that the stories I wanted to tell would be met with either total disregard, or worse: ire and derision. Especially since I had zero intention of feeding into the stereotypes that seemed to be "acceptable" when it came to portraying Black people in literature.

Would people even *want* to read stories about kids like me? Would they be as interested in our joys and triumphs as they seemed to be in our oppression and pain? I wanted to write about Black kids *living* and *loving*. Winning. Facing down obstacles and utilizing their gifts to save the day.

This was stuff I hadn't ever seen in books. At least not the books I was exposed to. Did the absence of these things *really* mean people just weren't interested (as a publisher—or five—suggested when rejecting my manuscripts)?

These questions plagued me as I waited for my little book baby to make its way out into the world. And I still had a year and five months left to wait when I sat down in a movie theater seat on a Saturday in May 2016.

The latest Marvel Cinematic Universe film had just dropped: *Captain America: Civil War.* And from the opening scene, I was rapt. The plot was spectacular, the action pulse-pounding, and the relationships delightfully fraught. One thing I've always loved about the MCU portrayal of super heroes is that every single one is deeply complex and vividly human—even the ones who aren't human at all. And you *want* to know their backstories.

So when a dude in a black catsuit comes out of nowhere and lands on a roof to fight the bad guy, then chases him through traffic largely on foot . . . and *then,* when caught by the police, just straight up *removes* his helmet to reveal his identity (umm, did somebody say *badass?*), and everyone in the theater *clapped* . . .

It literally changed everything for me.

Fast forward to February 2018. For almost two years, we'd heard whispers that the coming *Black Panther* movie would have a mostly Black cast, which was unheard of in the super hero space. The film released two days after Valentine's Day and I didn't go see it. I was scared. Scared of feeling let down. Scared people weren't believing the hype . . . and even more scared that they *were* believing it and would wind up disappointed. My little book had come out four months prior, almost to the day, and though it sold well enough in the first week to make the *New York Times* bestseller list, it was gone from said list by week two, and I had no idea how sales were going.

What if this movie came out and "underperformed" as I'd

heard editors say when some superhyped "diverse" book failed to meet sales expectations? Would that *prove* no one wanted stories about Black people doing great things and, you know, effectually end my storytelling career before it could really begin?

It took me a month to go see it. A month of it being the number-one film week after week. And the theater was packed when we took our seats. I even heard a guy in the row behind us say it was his fourth time seeing the movie in the theater (and at $16 per ticket, that sounded like a big deal).

Black Panther did well, obviously. It's one of the highest-grossing films of all time.

But it's also *so* much more.

The Black Panther—aka T'Challa aka Chadwick Boseman—struck a match the moment he landed on that roof in 2016. But his solo film in 2018 is what lit the fire of a revolution. People from *all* backgrounds got right on board with the Black king of a tiny fictional nation in East Africa, fighting to protect his country and its people from his cousin, an American-raised Black anarchist. There were only two white people who got significant screen time. Kids across the globe wanted to be the Black Panther and have super strength, speed, and catlike reflexes.

At long last, we were seeing Black excellence on-screen, in front of *and* behind the camera: The costume and production designers won highly coveted Oscars for their work. We saw a Black man—whose royal guard was made up of all Black women—rule with patience and integrity. We saw a wickedly witty Black girl genius and inventor (Shuri *really* changed my life, but we'll save that story for a different foreword). And best of all, we saw what Black people could do. Make.

Be.

And it changed us all.

Which is why this book exists. As I mentioned earlier, you hold in your hands a collection of essays from a vast array of Black people—from the man who raised enough money to pay for over seventy thousand kids to see the film in theaters to the beautiful woman who played a red-clad warrior of the Wakandan royal guard, the Dora Milaje. All sharing stories of how their individual lives were impacted by this juggernaut of a motion picture.

Thanks to Marvel Studios' *Black Panther*, I not only felt seen (finally!), but I also felt like I got the permission I needed to take up space. To tell the stories of my heart. To step out and make noise about things that don't align with the ideas put forth in the founding documents of this country, especially when it comes to people who look like me.

As you read, I hope you're reminded of all the ways this history-making film impacted you.

Wakanda forever.

DREAMS OF WAKANDA

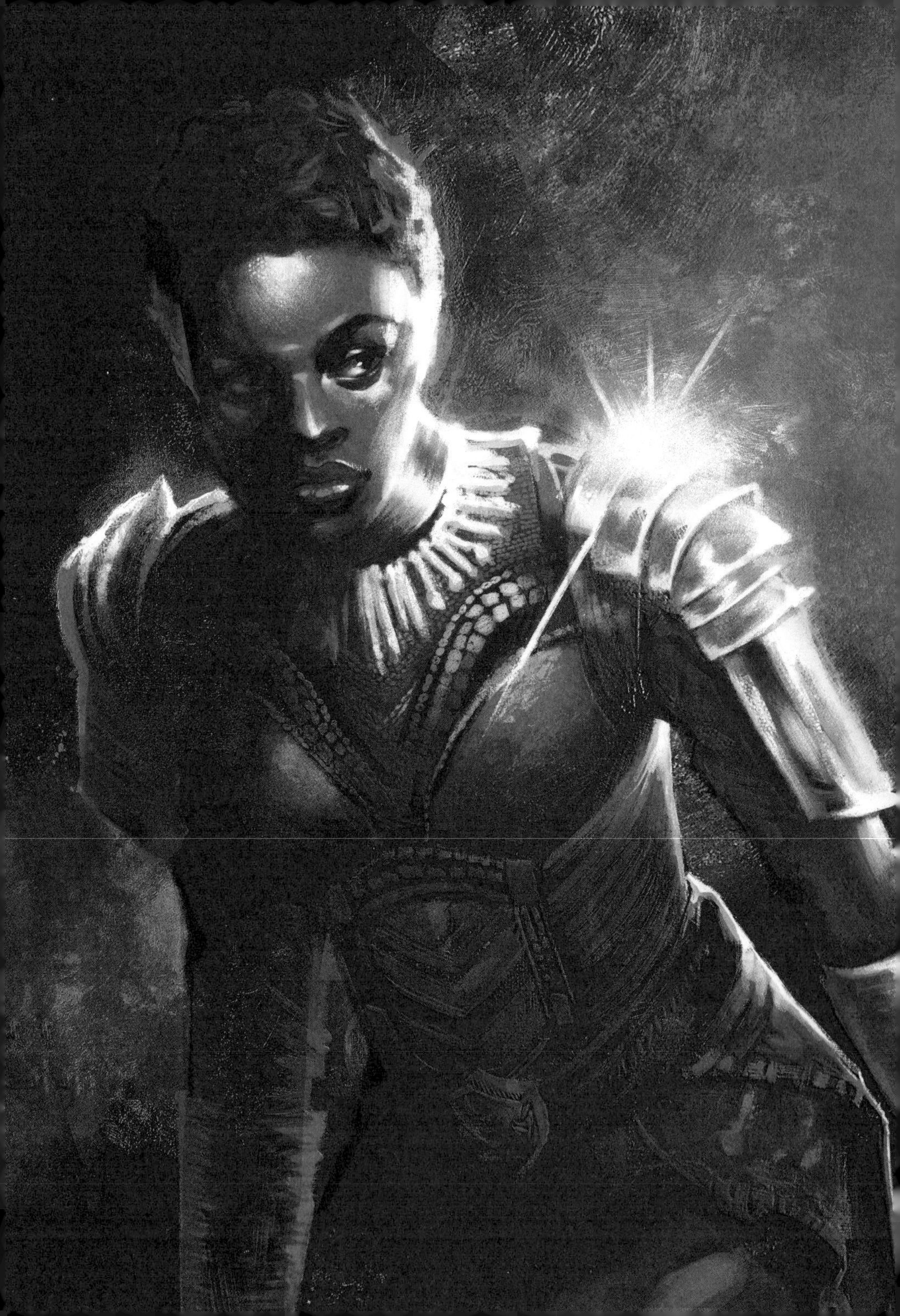

MEET ME IN WAKANDA: EMBRACING UNITY FROM PITTSBURGH TO DOHA

———————————◇———————————

Yona Harvey, award-winning poet,
contributor to Marvel Comics' *Black Panther:
World of Wakanda* and *Black Panther & the Crew*

THE ACE HOTEL of Pittsburgh delivered an early winter missive: "Marvel's much anticipated *Black Panther* movie premieres on February 16, and we're ready to celebrate. Join sarah huny young (AMERICAN WOMAN, *The Root 100*), Damon Young (*Very Smart Brothas, GQ*), and just a few (hundred) of our closest friends as *darkness spreads* from *Wakanda* to East Liberty." Though the Ace was the venue, the celebration was the brainchild of huny and her cousin Damon. At the time of organization, no one had seen the film, but spirits were as high as the optimism. The Marvel Cinematic Universe teasers and official film trailers had been effective. Not only would people turn out in numbers to view the movie, but they would also attend parties and movie theater lobby socials decked out in full Wakanda regalia.

I mentioned the Ace event to my BFFs in the DMV, and to my delight, they decided a road trip to Pittsburgh was in order. Like other cities around the world, the city where I lived would temporarily transform its venues and domiciles into the imagined African country of Wakanda. Because Wakanda lived in the hopes and dreams of people's imaginations, there were no boundaries on how people might dress and show their love for the popular comic book turned major motion picture. One of my BFFs had a toddler and asked if I could secure a babysitter. A close friend in Pittsburgh (also attending the party) said her daughter was available, and I felt grateful for the small, reliable, loving network of Black women down for the cause. Domestic missions accomplished, the social mission of dressing in style commenced. I pulled my outfit, which I'd purchased the previous year from an African braiding and dress shop owner who'd emigrated to Pittsburgh from the Congo. My BFF's husband, J, was from Kenya, and so the couple's outfits came from there.

I can't verify the origins of all the attire I saw that night, but the Ace Hotel's gym was awash in colorful prints, close haircuts, neatly oiled braids, and locks of many lengths and thicknesses. The vibe was unpretentious and welcoming. When the brother at the door couldn't find my e-ticket verification on his spreadsheet, he shrugged. "There're so many names," he said jovially, and waved us all in. A mix of tunes blared from the DJ's speakers, and later in the evening a crew of African drummers (no country or technique identified or sweated) gathered everyone in a large circle. A freestyle moment ensued, and my BFF nodded to her husband to show the good people how they do it in Kenya. Seconds later, he was at the center of the circle getting the respect his dancing deserved.

I'll admit I'd been kind of nervous at first, inviting a Kenyan native to an American-hosted Wakanda party. Even though J's only ever shown respect in our conversations across cultures and perspectives, I worried he might notice something grossly offensive or out of place, something inauthentic maybe. As a young undergraduate student in Washington, DC, I was often shocked at the condescension and assumptions made occasionally by a few Black adults from the Caribbean and some African countries I encountered around town or during my travels. There was a perception that Black Americans were ignorant of geography and culture, overly Afrocentric, diasporically needy, unworldly, and naive. Even as recently as 2019 Zadie Smith praised Darryl Pinckney's writing as "a useful corrective to lazy American ideas of Pan-Africanism." I'd never heard Pan-Africanism described as "lazy" (overly romantic, maybe) and I hadn't realized that, once again, Black Americans were labeled as offering the worst version of views that uninformed people from any country can potentially hold. A quizzical eagerness to put us in our place and explain just how ignorant we were persisted; colonial whites and their descendants had been historically prone to the same thing.

But J had no criticisms that night. And when I spoke to him a few years later about his travels in Kenya after seeing the *Black Panther* film and attending not one but several Wakanda-themed parties in his beloved country, his enthusiasm was palpable: "Africans in Africa were shocked that we [were] united in celebrating us as one . . . and everyone who was not African had to pay attention and see this phenomenon."

Interesting word, "unity." I found it would come up again and again. Maybe the Black American imagination—giver of jazz, scratching, sampling, and William Holmes Borders–style preaching—casts a widening, unstoppable, flourishing spell. One of its great mysteries, its great astonishments, rests in the notion that it seemingly comes out of nowhere, out of nothing or very little materially speaking, out of necessity. As the old sermons and gospel songs proclaimed: a way out of no way. As someone who's been given the side-eye numerous times, I embrace the hope—and the decades of hard work that fed into it—of a utopic, unified, fantastical space. Of course, utopias don't exist. But to conjure one forces us to examine the shortcomings and inequities around the world that inspire the longing for it. Perhaps this is what unites not only the people of the African diaspora but also sci-fi and fantasy film and literature lovers. Why should the flawed and limited thinking of colonial powers and former enslavers (and those who've absorbed that thinking) limit us? Why should any of us feel ashamed of wanting a connection? Why should a homeless person, wanderer, or anyone exiled feel self-conscious about longing for a home? Do I sound too romantic? Maybe.

The older I become, the more I think not about who's "more African" or "Blacker" but about the feeling of limitlessness literature and films like *Black Panther* give the displaced. In an ideal world, everyone knows where they "come from," none of us get separated from our families because of war or the pursuit of better education or better jobs, and no countries have border conflicts. But as the old maxim goes, we do not live in an ideal world.

One space that completely surprised me as a Wakanda celebration hub was Doha, Qatar. Qatar categorizes the people of African descent who reside there in multiple ways. My longtime family friend Chanda Bates, for example, is considered "an African American expatriate who resides in Qatar." She recently shared a curious list of descriptions for me: "An African laborer from Kenya is considered a migrant worker," but a company vice president also from Kenya is an "expatriate." Because of its sponsorship policies, Qatar doesn't officially allow immigrants. And those people who are descendants of Africans brought to the country as slaves are considered Qatari.

Chanda, her husband, Damian Dourado, and their teenage son have lived in Doha for several years now and attended a huge *Black Panther* premiere party sponsored by a social group composed of African descendants throughout the region. Invitees were asked to wear "traditional African garb," and, just as in Pittsburgh, anticipation was high. Those who didn't wear traditional clothing sported their best Black Panther and Dora Milaje costumes. Attendees purchased high volumes of tickets in advance and subsequently sold out two movie theaters. Chanda wore a dress she had had custom-made in Doha of Ghanaian fabric, and Damian wore a daishiki his father gifted him from his home country of Tanzania. Their personal crew of partygoers included a hair braider, a driver, a self-described "dark-skinned" Filipina friend who was teased as a child in her native country because of her complexion, and a housekeeper. "For once, everyone was equal," Chanda recalled. "It was not based on the haves or have-nots. Everyone was welcomed, accepted, and made to feel they matter. It was a true celebration that continued even after the movie was over."

Since moving to Doha, Chanda and Damian have also made friends from Ethiopia, Morocco, Cameroon, and Nigeria. Qatar has a large Sudanese population as well. "A sense of pride and a collective feeling of unity was represented that evening . . . [it's] often not visible since everyone lives spread out throughout the country," Chanda said. These friends often trade stories about their experiences abroad and have become like family. "[The film] allowed us to celebrate our rich and diverse cultures together, but for Qataris and other groups of people to witness. People were asking questions about what was happening and why we were gathered." Interesting word, "witness." Without films like *Black Panther,* perhaps, it would have taken much longer for Qataris to recognize the diversity and complexity of Africans residing right next to them. Even the fact that Qataris were asking questions and revealing some curiosity about the gathering speaks to the film's influence. I'm not suggesting that these problems were solved with the release of a single film. But it's arguable that in some parts of the world, at least, discernible waves of conversation in an ocean of global dismissal can help prevent ethnic and cultural complexities from being completely obscured.

At the very least, conversations about the film have revealed once again how ignorant, illogical, and nonsensical racist thinking can be. Chanda and Damian describe Qatar, for instance, as a passport-prejudiced country. Your country of origin influences the way people treat you. Chanda is frequently mistaken for Kenyan or Sudanese until she begins speaking and her American accent is heard. It's an odd reversal of sorts for her. She was born in Harrisburg, Pennsylvania. She laughs brightly when she recounts the story of tutoring a group of ESL students in Doha, who told her, "Oh, you don't sound like Madea [the Tyler Perry character]." Yikes. This kind of misinformation regarding Black people in the United States and elsewhere reminds me of the huge responsibility the film industry has when hiring skilled and talented writers who can bring depth, insight, and wholeness to Black characters. It's a significant cultural contribution when Marvel hires writers like Ryan Coogler to write in the category of action film—a category perceived as unworthy, incapable, or void of nuance and surprising storytelling. This is a gross miscalculation because at the end of the day—love it or hate it—more people will view films set in the MCU than they will independent films like Coogler's own *Fruitvale Station*. And what a joy to witness how Coogler's cinematic sensibilities translate and overlap in two tonally divergent films—whether audiences are aware of that intersectionality or not. The abundance of films featuring white Americans insulates that part of the population from being reduced to characters like those in, say, the 1994 American comedy *Dumb and Dumber*. A greater distribution of films about Black Americans across categories would do the same for Blacks in the diaspora, keeping the Madea-like stereotypes at bay.

To that end, I asked Chanda if she'd felt nervous about the *Black Panther* film before she viewed it. Was she worried the film might disappoint? A self-described "action, super hero movie fanatic," Chanda says her only worry was that the industry was releasing too many super hero movies at the time and that they might not "do Black Panther justice." But she was pleasantly surprised.

"We clapped at the end of that movie," she says, "and everybody walked out with such a . . ." She searches for the right words.

And then Damian steps in, not to mansplain, but to help capture that elusive feeling. "So when I walked out of *Black Panther,*

I hadn't walked out of a movie with a feeling like that since my childhood. . . . I went to see one of the [Rocky films], right? And I walked out with, like, this adrenaline." He remembers thinking when he was a kid, "Yeah, I wanna be a boxer." He laughs at himself. "Ever since that [childhood experience] occurred," he says, "I had never walked out of another movie and had like a true feeling or a physical feeling about it." He explains, of course, he'd seen films that were good, but *Black Panther* inhabited a completely different emotional realm.

As my friends and I gathered our belongings from the Ace Hotel coat closet that night in Pittsburgh and braced ourselves for the cold awaiting us outside, we had no idea what a fantastic film would greet us that weekend. Like a futuristic dreamscape, Wakanda was already alive behind portals around the world. Whether they knew it or not, Ryan Coogler, Joe Robert Cole, and Stan Lee had triggered new conversations about displacement, found families, and home.

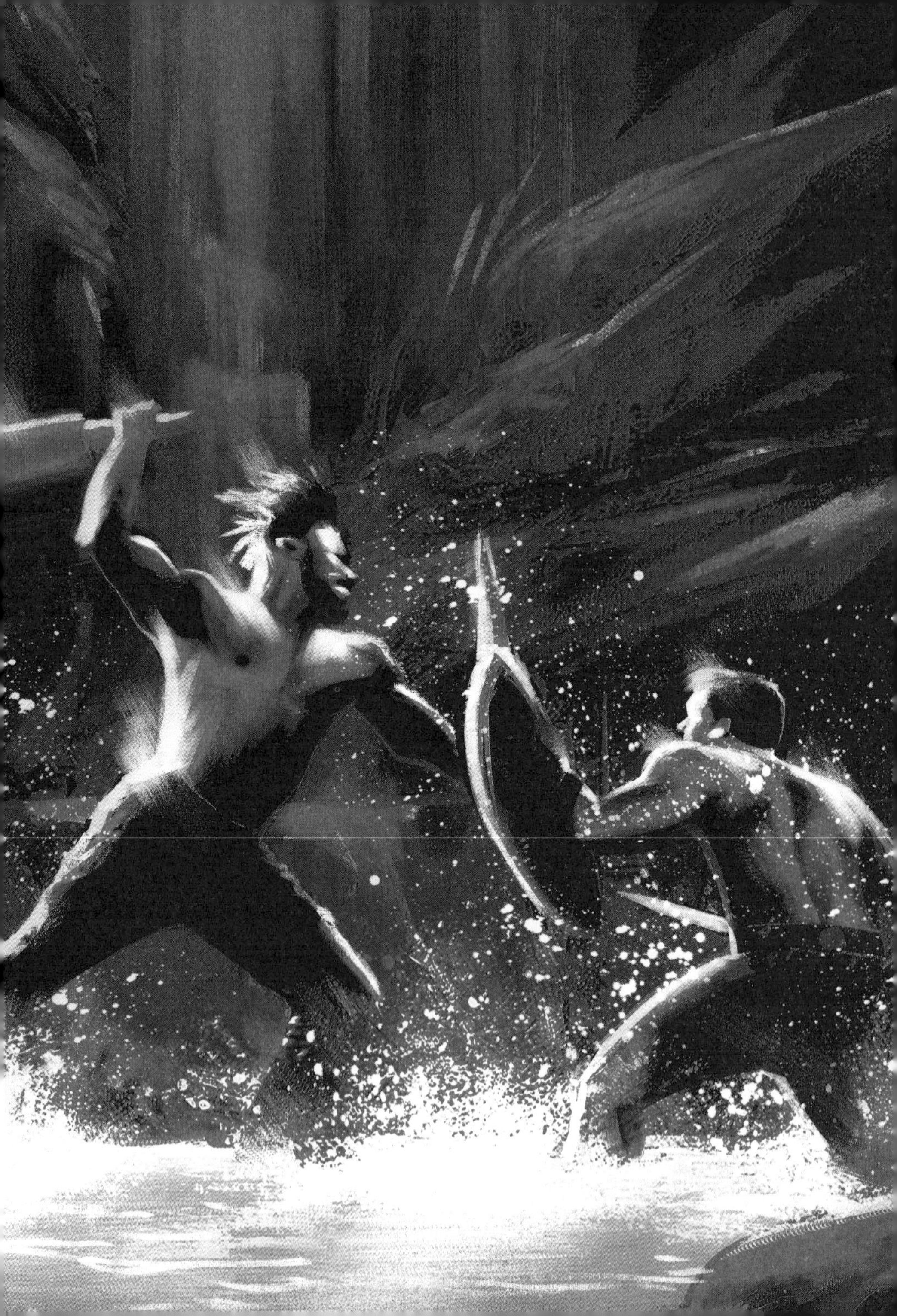

PANTHER PEDAGOGY: TEACHING *BLACK PANTHER* IN THE COLLEGE CLASSROOM

—◇◇—

Aaron C. Allen, professor of Roger Williams
University course "Wakanda Forever: The Racial Politics
in Marvel Studios' *Black Panther*"

I N THE FALL OF 2018, I taught a cultural studies course titled "Wakanda Forever: The Racial Politics in Marvel Studios' *Black Panther*." The class emerged out of a desire to develop a course on the cultural politics of race and racism that could garner student attention by focusing on a theme that had firmly established itself within popular culture. This was a necessary strategy born out of teaching at a predominately white liberal arts university that, like many other institutions of higher education, prioritizes student professional training. As a result, it is often difficult to convince students to enroll in courses on race and racism specifically, and those in the humanities more generally, without marketing them as cultural competency training for the workplace.

Black Panther seemed an obvious choice given that its release had garnered record-breaking success at the box office, a soundtrack debuting at number one, and numerous think pieces written by journalists and academics regarding its cultural impact. That said, I anticipated that a course on the film would at least pique students' curiosity enough for some to enroll. However, what began as a method of marketing a course to increase student enrollment—a practice that continues to unsettle me—turned into a series of lessons about the value of *Black Panther* for the college classroom. As I developed the course, it became evident to me that *Black Panther* co-writers Ryan Coogler and Joe Robert Cole offer a cast of characters that I could treat as co-instructors to teach students to wrestle with complex questions about Black identity and liberation.

In preparation for the Wakanda course, I came up with a series of questions and concerns in order to establish its academic legitimacy among my students. For instance, why use *Black Panther*'s fantastical world of Wakanda to discuss very real concerns over race and racism? Is *Black Panther* worthy of a semester-long course, and can it be a rigorous one? What does studying the film bring to bear on students' actual lives? By engaging students with the world of Wakanda, I provide a new way for them to engage with the politics of (anti-)Blackness. Too many lessons about Blackness begin with the documentation of Black suffering and premature death brought on by systemic racism. The topics of enslavement, Jim Crow policies, unequal educational opportunities, discriminatory practices in housing, the violation of voting rights, police brutality, and mass incarceration are all useful but very common entry points that instructors use to discuss the politics of anti-Black racism and Black resistance. However, consistently opening up such lessons with the brutality of these oppressive systems often results in students equating being Black with pure suffering. Discussions of race generally, and Blackness in particular, become ones always burdened by the heavy weight of oppression. *Black Panther* allowed me to flip the script by choosing as my entry point the joyous and creative spirit that propelled the film's anticipated release. This certainly was not my attempt to avoid the harsh realities that define Black struggle and resistance; rather, I was trying to enter into these lessons with a different emotional spirit. That is, I wanted to create a course that would invoke the same type of celebratory feelings as those felt around *Black Panther*'s release. The type of energy that inspired philanthropist Frederick Joseph to raise over $50,000 to take Harlem children to see the film in theaters for free, something that sparked similar campaigns throughout the United States—a practice popularly referred to as the #BlackPanther-Challenge. As my own personal challenge, I wanted to take the vibrancy that *Black Panther* invoked in audiences and create a course with a similarly vibrant tone. By choosing to build a course around a super hero film written by and about Black people, I was choosing to prioritize the life and energy that this representation produced.

However, I do want to note that the joy that emanated from *Black Panther*'s Black representation is certainly not enough to build a sixteen-week course around. While the film is lauded for its display of Black excellence both behind and in front of the camera, I fear that by merely focusing on the benefits of representation students miss the complex lessons that *Black Panther* offers. In fact, the majority of the students who enroll in the course already arrive with an understanding of the importance of diverse representation, and most, if not all, enter the classroom believing that this is *the* most important lesson of *Black Panther*.

Rather, *Black Panther* demands a semester-long course because of its willingness to explore the complexities of racial identity and different strategies for achieving Black freedom. At the time of *Black Panther*'s release, no other Marvel Cinematic Universe property had engaged with the politics of Blackness so explicitly. In fact, *Black Panther* is arguably the first film to enjoy the massive blockbuster success expected of the super hero genre while simultaneously tackling the complexities of race, identity, and colonialism head-on. As a result, my students are given the time to sufficiently examine the film for its lessons. Students are expected to view, discuss, and write about *Black Panther* with the same intellectual rigor as material typically considered more "academic."

To help facilitate this level of engagement, I situate the film alongside work produced by cultural theorists, historians, philosophers, and journalists discussing issues such as Black nationalism, colonialism, Black feminism, Afrofuturism, and African-descended peoples' notion of "home." Students are required to collaborate on a scripted presentation that identifies thematic connections between *Black Panther* and a book by African American cultural historian Saidiya Hartman entitled *Lose Your Mother*. Hartman's book recounts her voyage along Ghana's slave routes in an attempt to recover history and kin. Hartman finds herself with an unrecoverable past, a stranger to both America and Africa. Students are tasked with placing *Black Panther* in direct conversation with this text by identifying ideas that connect the two. Students are then given the opportunity to showcase their analyses by inviting guests to attend their small symposium-style presentations. Ultimately, I assign analytically driven projects like this to disrupt any misconception among my students that the course is an opportunity to act as amateur movie reviewers or an occasion to debate *Black Panther*'s entertainment value, potential plot holes, degree of continuity within the larger MCU franchise, or other points of discussion that divert from the cultural import of the film.

The course's primary strategy for getting students to engage in a deeper analysis of *Black Panther* is to reframe the way they view the film's characters. Students are expected to view *Black Panther*'s heroes and villains as more than just characters in the film; indeed, they are teachers of the course. Framing *Black Panther*'s primary characters as co-instructors treats the world of Wakanda as an extension of the classroom rather than as a self-contained film. T'Challa, Killmonger, Nakia, and the others are not simply an ensemble of characters driving the plot of *Black Panther,* but rather bona fide teachers possessing their own vision for how we might think through Black identities as well as the multifaceted ideas of Black freedom. Rather than these characters delivering lectures in front of the class, however, their words, choices, and actions in the film are their method and practice of teaching. Below I share some of the lessons that co-instructors T'Challa, Erik "Killmonger" Stevens (N'Jadaka), and Nakia bring to the course.

PROFESSOR T'CHALLA

A point of internal conflict for the titular character, King T'Challa, is whether to open up Wakanda so that the rest of the

world, particularly Black people impoverished by ongoing racism, can benefit from its technological resources. T'Challa's internal struggle teaches students about the complexities of Black
identity. On the one hand, his status as a king, possessing a
wealth of resources untouched by Western colonialism, explains
the feelings of pride among many Black people throughout the
world. He is an example of positive Black representation given
his status as both super hero and king. In this way, we learn that
T'Challa's home is, for many Black peoples around the globe, a
utopia within an otherwise anti-Black world. On the other hand,
T'Challa's status as king is not pure. We learn that for many
other Black people, T'Challa's role as king preserves a monarchi-
cal system based on ordering society along a social hierarchy
rather than an actual transformation of it. (If there are royals in
Wakanda, surely there are peasants.) Hartman writes in *Lose
Your Mother,* "The slave does not enjoy the rights and entitle-
ments of 'royals' and 'nobles,' those who are the legitimate heirs
of lineage. Love extends the cover of belonging and shrouds the
slave's origins."* Hartman reminds us that Black people throughout the world are descendants of enslaved Africans and it is this
ancestry that has produced a community of strength, creativity,
and resilience among them, *not* a lineage of nobility. From this
perspective, we learn that the royalty that King T'Challa possesses is nothing to desire or identify with. Unlike the film's end-

---

* Saidiya Hartman, *Lose Your Mother: A Journey Along the Atlantic Slave Route* (New York: Farrar, Straus, and Giroux, 2007), 87.

ing, the course does not seek to resolve for students T'Challa's internal conflict over his role as king or the future of Wakanda. Rather, in our class T'Challa asks students to embrace the tension that he finds within himself as king. Doing so holds much larger lessons about the complexities that shape the relationship between Black identity, belonging, and the meaning of true empowerment.

PROFESSOR ERIK "KILLMONGER" STEVENS (N'JADAKA)

Much has been written about the MCU's take on Killmonger. Some have celebrated him as a revolutionary antihero who seeks to unleash Wakanda's vibranium technology against the world's colonizers in order to liberate Black people, and all oppressed peoples, around the globe. He is interpreted as a Malcolm X–like figure who attempts to free his people from global oppression by any means necessary. Others have labeled him a villain, even if a tragic one. Critics see him as a rejected Wakandan who merely tries to reproduce the same type of Western imperial domination over the world, only in reverse. Critics often point to Killmonger's problematic declaration that the "sun will never set on the Wakandan empire" as a nod to a historical phrase used by Western imperial powers since the sixteenth century. Killmonger has even been cited as the primary reason, according to philosopher Christopher Lebron, that *"Black Panther* is not the movie we deserve." Lebron argues that Killmonger's story continues the "devaluation of black American men," as the film represents him as the most dangerous man in the world pitted against a more dignified form of Black African nobility.[*]

Rather than debate Killmonger's status as hero or villain, or argue whether we deserve a better treatment of him, the course frames him as varied, complex, and potentially without resolution. Even within the limitations of his narrative lie important lessons. Erik "Killmonger" Stevens (N'Jadaka) encourages students to appreciate the messiness of Black freedom struggles. On the one hand, Erik Stevens shows us the beauty of Black nationalism. Just as his orphan status inspires his connection with and desire to uplift Black people throughout the world, this sense of community and strength among African-descended people too emerges from a collective sense of being orphaned from the world. On the other hand, he also teaches us about the historical shortcomings of Black nationalism. We witness his violent treatment of women throughout the film, which begs us to consider the ways in which particular Black nationalist philosophies and freedom movements have ignored Black women and queer-identified folx. Ultimately, Killmonger encourages students to take his characterization and political ideologies as *both* redeemable *and* contemptible in order to teach important lessons about racism and resistance.

* Christopher Lebron, "*Black Panther* Is Not the Movie We Deserve," *Boston Review*, February 17, 2018, bostonreview.net/race/christopher-lebron-black-panther.

PROFESSOR NAKIA

Nakia offers students an introduction to Black feminism. Her teachings on the subject do not come merely as a result of her being a Black woman represented on-screen—too often the mere representation of Black women becomes equated with the practice of Black feminism. Rather, as Kimberlé Crenshaw's concept of intersectionality has taught us, Black feminism is not an identity but rather a framework to better analyze how different forms of oppression (e.g., racism, sexism, and colonialism) work together to impact groups of people differently, with Black women's experiences being central to this analysis.* As a spy for Wakanda's intelligence service, the War Dogs, Nakia is well-traveled and has certainly witnessed these intersecting forms of oppression firsthand. In the film, her Black feminist lessons are practiced, in part, through an early appeal for Wakanda to care for the most vulnerable throughout the world. We see Nakia and T'Challa stroll through a marketplace as she counsels him to consider sharing Wakanda's resources beyond its borders. "I have seen too many in need to turn a blind eye," she warns. We are left to imagine the details of what she has seen, although our

---

* See Kimberlé Williams Crenshaw's foundational essay on intersectionality, "Demarginalizing the Intersection of Race and Sex: A Black Feminist Critique of Antidiscrimination Doctrine, Feminist Theory and Antiracist Politics," *University of Chicago Legal Forum* 1, no. 8 (1989): 139–167.

introduction to her character earlier in the film hints at the brutality she has witnessed, particularly among those trapped at the intersection of multiple forms of oppression. On a rescue mission in Nigeria, Nakia is seated in the back of a truck alongside several women and a child held captive by militants just before she, alongside T'Challa and Okoye, rescues them. Absent the plentiful resources available to Nakia as a Wakandan, she is just as vulnerable as the other women in the back of that truck. It is there Nakia invites us to see what she sees—the strength and vulnerability particular to Black women: an important foundational lesson for Black feminism.

Ultimately, the course understands that *Black Panther*'s characters are vehicles that drive us to understand much broader questions about Blackness as an identity, as political philosophy, and as a mode of creativity. Treating T'Challa, Erik "Killmonger" Stevens (N'Jadaka), and Nakia (among others) as my co-instructors asks students to remain open to the lessons they are trying to teach us through their stories. It requires that they watch, listen, and consider these characters' perspectives with the same attention they would give to a lecture I might deliver or a class discussion I might facilitate. The course is not simply about understanding the film in more sophisticated ways; rather, it treats *Black Panther* and its characters as a way of better understanding racial politics in our world.

A FINAL ASSIGNMENT

It is with the above in mind that I ask my students to develop a speculative analysis paper on *Black Panther* as a final assignment. The idea is that once students have learned the many lessons that its characters teach in and through the narrative, they are given the opportunity to dream up their own lessons concerning the politics of race and racism. The assignment consists of two parts. Part one asks students to write a piece of fan fiction that further develops and/or challenges the lessons taught by the film's story and characters. Using the story that Coogler and Cole created as a template, students speculate on alternative or future directions for the film, presenting it as a piece of literature or screenplay. Part two then asks students to write a self-analysis of their speculative work. This second part requires that they draw on course materials and outside research to explain how their creative choices make a social, political, and cultural comment on broader issues pertaining to power, oppression, and/or political resistance. Students' speculative analyses offer an opportunity for them to creatively engage with issues of racial politics by using the world of Wakanda, while compelling them to think carefully about how these imaginative choices are informed by broader cultural ideas around race and racism. This not only forces my students to take responsibility for their thoughts and words (and actions), but it also allows them to unburden themselves of the belief that they are the sole creator of them. The assignment gives them an opportunity to reflect on how they are guided by broader social and cultural assumptions that align with or depart from ideologies that are as deeply embedded in society as they are in our psyche. The goal of the assignment is for students to be self-reflective about how their imaginations are deeply tied to racial politics and give them an opportunity to use *Black Panther* to envision an alternative, more equitable world.

When introducing the assignment, I remind my students that Wakanda is a result of what Robin D. G. Kelley has called freedom dreaming—the practice of imagining worlds with freer possibilities than our current one offers.[*] Freedom dreaming has always been integral to Black liberatory projects. Descendants of Africans in the Americas have always set out to envision and create spaces and lives beyond the reach of white supremacy. Historian N.D.B. Connolly suggests that we can locate Wakanda's historical roots in the real-life imaginings of Black utopias. He draws a through-line from early sixteenth-century maroon colonies—settlements established by African descendants, often alongside indigenous groups, as a way to escape slavery—to the imaginative nation of Wakanda.[†]

Tapping into our imaginations is precisely how freedom dreams are made manifest. I ask my students to recognize how the stories they create reflect underlying philosophies that con-

[*] Robin D. G. Kelley, *Freedom Dreams* (Boston: Beacon Press, 2002).

[†] N.D.B. Connolly, "How 'Black Panther' Taps into 500 Years of History," *The Hollywood Reporter*, February 16, 2018, hollywood reporter.com/heat-vision/black-panther-taps-500-years-history -1085334.

tribute to the formation of our material world. The assignment in and of itself is certainly not an act of social justice and must not be perceived as one, but it is an opportunity for students to spend a sustained amount of time envisioning what justice looks like beyond the constraints of practicality, which so often impede our creativity. More than just a paper, it is an opportunity for students to use the world of *Black Panther* to critically reenvision how the world around them makes space for Black futures and to remain attuned to the ways that it currently does not. Ultimately, the refrain "Wakanda forever" is an implicit demand for us to never stop imagining alternative lives and affirming worlds. For us to forever embrace the possibility of a world apart from the one we inhabit. It is my hope that my "Wakanda Forever" course demonstrates the power of imagining fantastical worlds and what that can tell us about our own. While I set out to attract students to my class by using the popularity of *Black Panther,* what has emerged is a semester-long relationship built between the film's characters, my students, and myself. Each run through the film, each scene, is an opportunity for reflection about broader ideas pertaining to the politics of Blackness and questions concerning the Black diaspora.

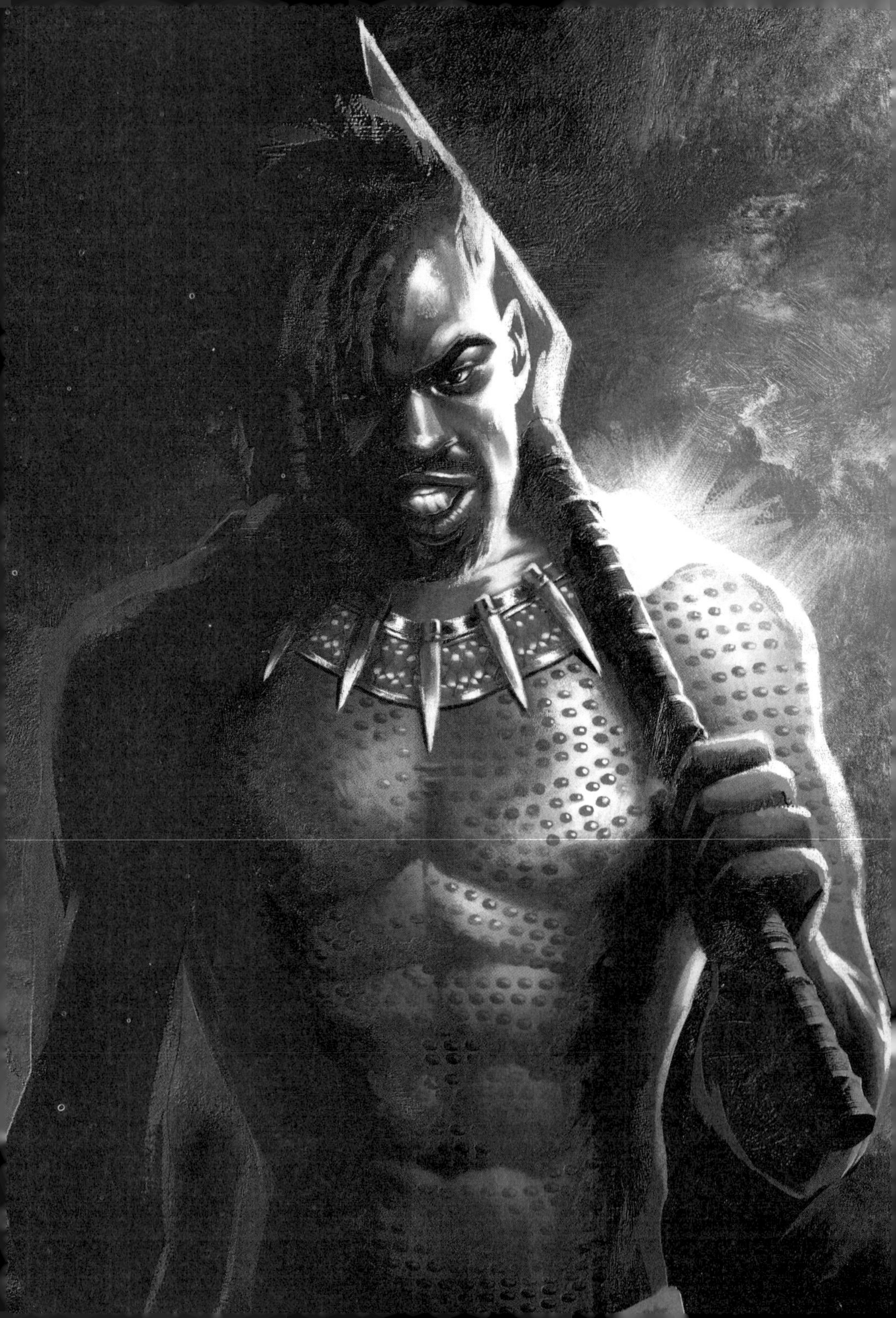

THEY WILL SAY YOU ARE LOST:
THE SORROW OF N'JADAKA

◇◇

Frederick Joseph, award-winning author,
activist, and educator, creator of the
#BlackPantherChallenge

FROM ITS CINEMATOGRAPHY to its creative direction, the film *Black Panther* is undoubtedly a beautiful work of art. But where its true genius and beauty shine is in its ability to unapologetically capture the tragic truth of people who are often unseen. People such as the film's antagonist, Killmonger. His character asks viewers to grapple with concepts that many find difficult, such as the fact that humans are complex, and therefore multiple things can be true about them. Killmonger is a prime example of this. While his actions were wrong, they were rooted in a Black American pain and sadness that felt almost as familiar as an old photo of myself. He is a villain born of his life as a victim.

In many ways, Killmonger was a poisonous fruit that grew in a rotten garden. While we must avoid eating the fruit, it's just as important that we understand that the fruit did not plant itself. The seeds of Killmonger's anguish and anger were sowed by the waters of the Middle Passage and everything that followed. On his surface, *Black Panther*'s villain is simply a man fueled by rage and revenge, but at his core, he is a boy drifting in a storm of violence, anti-Blackness, and misogynoir. To understand Killmonger, you must first understand the systemic trauma of the boy inside of him. The drifting boy who grew to be a man who was never found.

For a person to be found, they must first take the often difficult step of accepting that they are lost. But *difficult* is an understatement when being lost exists at the center of who some people are. I am one of those people. A person belonging to a tribe without a country, a family without a home. Wandering through a land of fog controlled by people who look nothing like me, surrounded by monuments to them, built by hands that look like my mother's, her mother's, and mine. Monuments not only to my people being lost, but also to my people being taken. The homes we weren't allowed to own, schools that don't teach our history, prisons that try to erase us. These monuments symbolizing the trauma many of us drag around like a rusting anchor.

That trauma is a book pre-written for generations of Black people in the United States. A book that radicalized Killmonger, and his father, N'Jobu. A book filled with pages they had planned to burn.

In seeing the complexities and angst of Killmonger, I think back to my childhood. Most of my youth was spent living in government-run public housing complexes, or as we call them in New York, "the projects." They were large, uniform brown brick buildings filled with apartments that were cream-colored, and also uniformly neglected by the city officials who were responsible for their upkeep. Overpoliced playgrounds, urine-filled elevators, and pipes coated with lead. While there was joy and love to be found among the families who occupied those walls, there was also an immense feeling of struggle. Most of us had been born into life in the projects, as our parents before us, and their parents before them—a life from which there was very little opportunity to escape.

We had done nothing to deserve this life. If there was a wrong or crime committed, it was simply the audacity of being Black in an anti-Black country. Generations trying their best to survive, the remnants of four hundred years of systemic oppression.

I recall being a young boy when my mother explained to me what had happened to Emmett Till, hoping to avoid a similar fate befalling her own young Black son. I remember asking her a question that seemed simple but was loaded with the weight of everything that was heavy in our lives: "Why does America hate us?" She stared at me for a moment; the heartbreak in her eyes was not obvious to me then, but it is now. In the years since that moment, I've learned all too well the sadness of having to explain to a young Black child what place they hold on the long list of the United States' sins.

My mother tried her best to explain the evils that she herself could not fully comprehend. But as she told tales of cotton fields and mentioned names like Jim Crow, I became fixated not on *hows* and *whys,* but rather *whos* and *wheres.* If we are not simply a people of struggle, then who are we? If this place is not meant for us, then where are we supposed to be?

I began to look around and wonder to myself whether most of the people living as we were, our tribe, felt as I did. Were we all out of place, like fish flying above the ocean? Were we all dreaming of escaping the fog and monuments—dreaming of being found? During my years in college, that dream boiled over into a well of emotions that were unshakable. My urge to be elsewhere was now only surpassed by my anger with this place that had taken so much from my people. College gave me the chance to learn more about the United States, and the more I learned, the more I felt lost. The more lost I felt, the angrier and more radicalized I became. There was a Killmonger growing inside of me.

I couldn't stand how much hate was burning inside of me. The desire to be somewhere that made more sense, somewhere Black, had become a necessity. I was reminded of something my grandmother often said to me as a child: "When you lose something, including yourself, go back to where you began." So I retraced our steps and went to the place where I hoped I would finally feel at home.

The first time I visited Africa—Kenya, to be exact—I was in my early twenties. My uncle had done research and found that our ancestors had migrated from there to West Central Africa during the transatlantic slave trade. They were then stolen by white colonial settlers and brought to the shores of stolen land that would eventually become the United States of America. While I was interested in eventually visiting West Central Africa, my compass was pointed directly toward what I felt was the very beginning. It was the Kenyan rivers and sun that flowed through my veins and kissed my skin to give it its hue.

It was a trip I had saved money for years to take, and yet still couldn't afford. But with the racial strife taking place in the United States at that time, I knew I *had* to leave, for my own well-being. So I sold all of my possessions that people were willing to buy. Coats, sneakers, videogame systems—I even donated my own blood for money. And I bought my ticket.

There are many things that stand out about my first trip to Africa, but the thing I always recall was the first leg of my plane ride there. At the time it was the longest flight I had been on, and there aren't enough words to describe how anxious I was. But what I was anxious about had nothing to do with the flight. I would compare it more to the feeling of the first day of school as a child. You've thought about the day for weeks, your outfit is ready the night before, but on the way all you can think about is whether you'll be received well. Will the other children like you? Have they been waiting to see you as much as you've been waiting to see them? After so long, will they remember you?

What if, like the United States, Kenya—or any country in Africa, for that matter—was not meant for me? Maybe I was destined to be lost forever.

My worries must have been obvious, because an older man who was sitting next to me asked whether I was okay. I immediately lied, "I'm fine." To which he responded with a smile, "Your palms tell a different story." I looked down at my hands and lightly chuckled; my palms had sweat enough to flood the Nile River. Before I could say anything else, the man continued, "Why don't we chat? You seem like someone who makes good conversation." I looked at him for a moment, realizing I had not paid attention to him before, so much so that it was as if I were seeing him for the first time.

He had a deep voice that, coupled with his accent, made his words sound like music, and a beard with large flecks of gray in it that told the story of a man who had the privilege of time, a privilege so rarely afforded to men such as myself where I came from. "I want to grow old enough to have a beard like that someday," I thought to myself. But what made me oblige his request for conversation was his eyes. His eyes seemed both kind and wise, like whatever I said would be filtered through good faith and experience.

We ended up speaking for hours; he told me all about his family, his work, and his home country, Iran. I reciprocated him trusting me with so many details of his life by telling him all about mine as well, including why I was heading to Kenya and what was making me so nervous. Beyond brief pleasantries, he didn't comment much on the worries, trauma, or anger I had shared. It was as if he knew I just needed someone to listen—and listen he did. Though I hadn't realized it, I was no longer nervous. But his calming presence was not the only gift he gave me that day. As we walked off the plane he said something that not only colored my entire trip but also helped shape the rest of my life: "Home is not something that can be taken from you. Your shared blood is a birthright. You all deserve more than heartache." Then with a hug and a wish of safe travels, he was gone.

As much as I've tried, I can't remember his name. It's interesting how some of the people who make the greatest impact are the people who float in distant memories that are hard to reach. Like the chorus of a song you know all the words to, but can't remember who wrote them. I'll never forget his face, nor the melodic words he added to my life. Words that brought me the peace I needed to fully experience setting my feet on African soil for the first time. Words that helped send me home.

The moment the plane touched down on the tarmac in Nairobi my emotions cracked open like a bottle flung against a sea of rocks. It all poured out of me: the generations spent in the projects, the years of overpolicing, the days wondering why they hated me, the hours watching the news call us anything but our names. It all came out right there, as I looked out the window and saw rows of planes bearing the Kenyan flag and airport staff who looked like me and the millions of our family members who were back home. I closed my eyes and took a deep breath, almost as if I were breathing for the first time in my life. Maybe I was.

My time in Kenya wasn't spent going on extravagant safaris, staying at luxurious hotels, or eating at Michelin-starred restaurants. Most of my days were filled with wandering through the streets, asking questions, and taking in culture. I slept in hostels and ate at small discreet places. I wasn't there to exist in the largest way possible; I was there to simply exist unapologetically. If I had to describe my trip, I would call it perfectly imperfect. There were people I met who scoffed at my being there, people who called me "Yankee" and other variations of "American." Variations of the idea that I didn't belong, the realizations of my fear that I would be lost forever. But there were also the children who would run up to me and ask if I wanted to kick a ball around with them, as if I were their older cousin they hadn't seen in too long. There were the taxi drivers who were eager to give me the history of every neighborhood we drove through and the best places to live, "just in case you decide to move here." Most of all, there was the older woman who kept one of the hostels I stayed at. We shared a pot of mint tea in the common area my first night as we compared notes on growing up in our different worlds. When I woke up the next morning, there was a note under my door with various sayings in Swahili to help me in conversation, and under them two words every Black person in the world deserves to hear: "Welcome home."

The opportunity to be in a place where your skin and culture aren't criminalized is a privilege far too many take for granted. That trip, that moment in time, not only rejuvenated me but in many ways saved my life. Saved me from becoming the embodiment of the historical and daily tragedies that plague Black America. Saved me from becoming the lost man I saw years later in *Black Panther*.

As I watched the film, there was one moment in particular that broke my heart. After believing that he has killed his cousin T'Challa and taking the Heart-Shaped Herb to gain the heightened abilities of the Black Panther, Killmonger goes through a ritual that allows him to visit the astral dimension, where he can commune with the dead. The first thing I noticed immediately was that unlike T'Challa, who had visited the astral dimension earlier in the film, where it was represented by a beautiful African plain, Killmonger's visit to the astral dimension was represented by the Oakland public housing apartment he grew up in. But if you look closely through the windows of that apartment, you can see that the astral African plain exists outside. I took this symbolism a few ways. First, the apartment represents the trauma and rage that Killmonger is still trapped in. Second, the juxtaposition of the apartment and the African plain symbolizes the dreams and pain of Black people such as myself, who yearn for a place that seems so close, yet so far.

The spirit of Killmonger's father, N'Jobu, comes to him, and as soon as he does, Killmonger becomes a young boy again. He becomes N'Jadaka, the same lost boy who walked into that apartment and found his father lying dead after he was killed by his brother, T'Chaka, then the king of Wakanda and the Black Panther. Their conversation hurt me in ways that reminded me of my mother trying to answer my question as to why America hated us. N'Jobu explains to his son why, as a child whose father was Wakandan but whose mother was African American, he might not be welcomed in the isolationist Wakanda. Which speaks to why, earlier in the conversation, young N'Jadaka refers to Wakanda as his father's home, as opposed to his. A reflection of the anxiety that African Americans are not welcome either in the United States or in countries in Africa—the fear that we have no home.

N'Jobu then comments on the fact that his young son has seemingly shed no tears for his lost father, to which N'Jadaka shakes his head and replies, "Everybody dies—it's just life around here." N'Jobu's eyes begin to fill with tears as he says, "Well, look at what I've done. I should have taken you back long ago. Instead, we are both abandoned here."

When the camera pans back to his son, instead of young N'Jadaka, we see Killmonger, who wipes away a single tear. His sadness has seemingly been consumed by the rage of his trauma, as he responds to his father, "Maybe your home's the one that's lost. That's why they can't find us." Tears roll down N'Jobu's face as he lowers his head, as if coming to the full realization of how far gone his son is. How his radicalization was not coupled with joy, which will lead him down a path of both internal and external destruction.

I, too, wept for lost N'Jadaka.

Killmonger was a character who represented generations of the same trauma that lived inside me. A man who was so lost that he found himself using the same tools the masters had used to subjugate us to try to free us—violence against Black women, violence against our lost cousins, waging war against our home. As the great writer and activist Audre Lorde said, "The master's tools will never dismantle the master's house."

There are only two tools that can truly liberate anyone, both of which I found in Kenya—hope and healing.

To understand the genius that is *Black Panther,* you must first understand the tragedy of Killmonger as an indictment of the United States' sins. The realities of a young Black man who wandered through a land of fog and monuments standing as a testament to his struggle, a boy who fell into the pitfalls of a country where it often feels as if hope and healing are luxuries not afforded to people such as us. He is a villain, but he is also a victim of the systems that created him. He is a poisonous fruit, but he is not the person who tended the rotten garden.

N'Jadaka is the boy I wish I could have met on a plane with flecks of gray in my beard and eyes that received him through good faith and experience, so I could let him know he didn't have to be lost. So I could tell him, "You deserve more than heartache."

So, maybe, he could finally feel found.

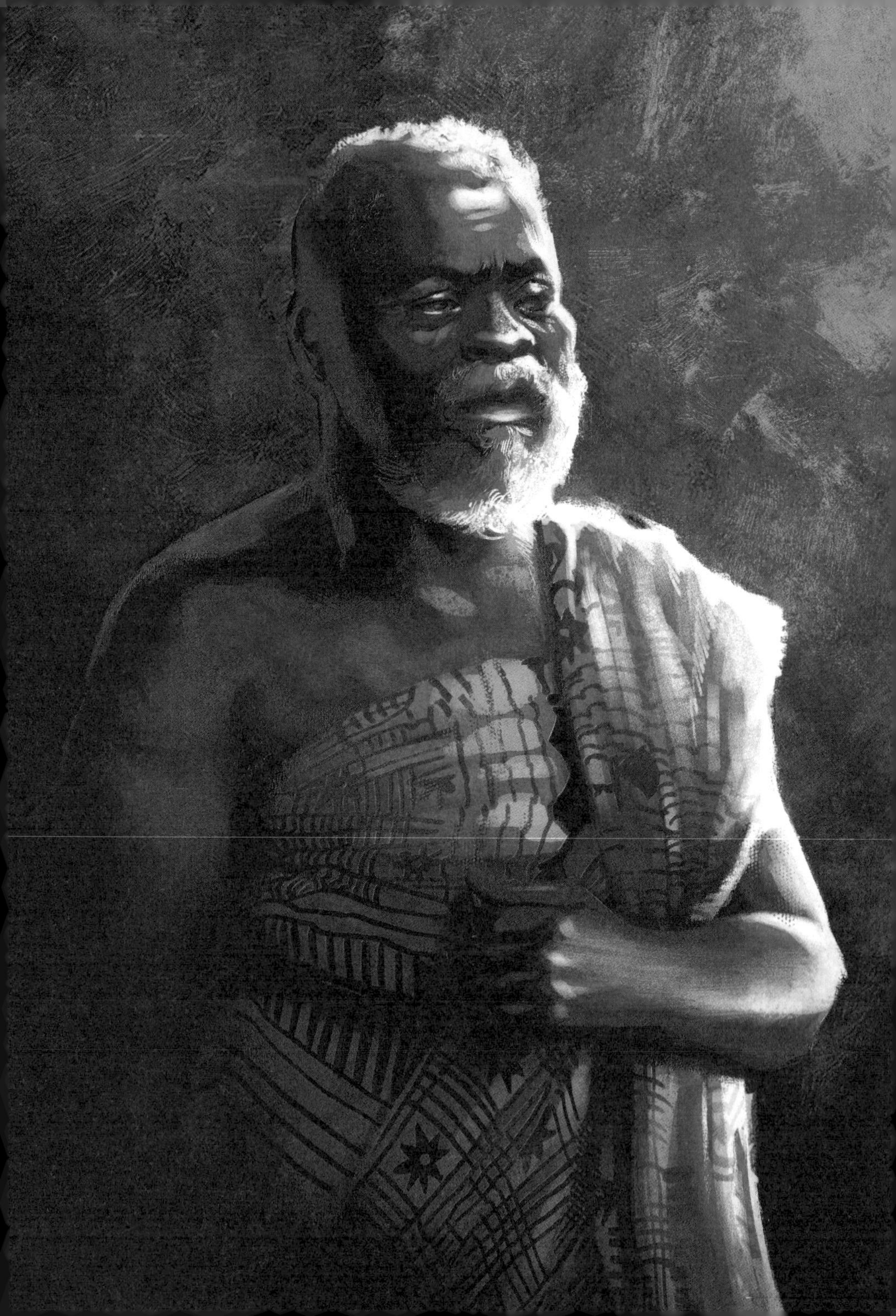

THE METAPHORIC QUALITY OF VIBRANIUM

Tre Johnson, writer and journalist,
race, culture, and politics

At the height of the summer's racial reckoning in 2020, I joined a group of friends to march the streets of Philadelphia in protest of the brutal slayings of George Floyd, Ahmaud Arbery, and Breonna Taylor, the latest casualties on a list that's long been too extensive to recite in conversation, march, writing, or protest. As we beat our feet from the steps of the city's art museum, around the City Hall rotary, and up Broad Street, we walked among a rainbow coalition of people of all races, hues, and identities, a phalanx of masked people peacefully pounding the pavement in protest. The hum of peace, mourning, exhaustion, hope, determination, and community filled my body and the bodies around me. I took it all in: the hastily made protest signs; the self-organized people who dispensed water bottles, hand sanitizer, and masks; the children straddling the shoulders of adults; the youth buoyantly moving along the wave of the crowd. Underneath my feet I felt the vibrations of thousands of feet moving less in physical unison and more in movement. By then, we'd taken in so much, particularly Black people. It was late June 2020 and the pandemic had fully settled in, sapping community strength and widening the chasm of inequalities we already knew about. The ways we'd always felt connected—through church, through the internet, through barbershops and basketball courts—were dismally, despairingly broken. Public health press conferences maligned Black people's desire and ability to communally gather, singling out a population that had already felt singularly uniquely impacted by COVID-19 in the country. And then, the killings. And then, the video. And then, naturally, necessarily, the marching.

It was different in 2017. In 2017, along with the now familiar viral images of murder, a counterpoint was building energy among Black people, for Black people. As trailer after trailer dropped for *Black Panther,* an energy and an excitement grew among Black people watching each one. The anticipation of *Black Panther*'s release was a timely distraction from the changing of the guard that was beginning to happen over at 1600 Pennsylvania Avenue around that time, becoming an unlikely but necessary antidote to the country's changing political climate. In 2017, America was still discussing the notions of its goodness and innocence without meaningfully asking the people most familiar with those answers to weigh in very often. But the film, with its promise of an independent, empowered futuristic Black society, seemingly unburdened from the daily assaults of what it meant to be Black in America, gathered an energy around it that was nearly palpable. While most of the conversations around *Black Panther* were about seeing a Black super hero lead in a genre that had long lagged in representation, in the heart of the movie and its universe sat the preciousness of what vibranium meant to both fictional and real Black people.

Absorb, store, and release. Buried in the heart of every Black person is a sliver of vibranium. How could anything else possibly be true? In Wakanda, vibranium runs through the people and the region like plasma, powering its homes and its culture. It's embedded in clothing and devices. At the core of the Black Panther's armor, vibranium charges the suit, adding more to T'Challa's already incredible inherent strength. It is Wakanda's greatest resource, second only to its people. Vibranium was perhaps the most unlikely thing to encounter as a mirror in a film that was more often talked about for the way it presented Black heroes on the big screen in such a grand fashion. Yet not everyone could be or wants to be a king or a super hero; most of us just want to be able to get by, be happy, and not have to absorb the innumerable slings and arrows that come with being Black Americans. Vibranium feels like the metaphorical distillation of what makes us us. What else could represent the ways that Black people have turned pain into power and used it for a collective good? The Black American experience has been about the unfathomable and beautiful ways we've absorbed, stored, and released the various energies that have assaulted and surrounded us since being forcibly brought to the North American shores centuries ago. For us, vibranium is putting a name to the thing we've used to develop our identity, our culture, and our future. Black people have absorbed so much, and have routinely held our heads up high even as progress toward acknowledging our humanity has been held up.

After all, what else would you call the ability to have endured the Edmund Pettus Bridge walk on 1965's "Bloody Sunday"? Or years earlier, with Nina Simone's 1963 creation and performance of "Mississippi Goddam"? In comedian Dick Gregory's 1964 memoir, he talks about taking the white-hot heat of racism and transmuting that into his comedy; how he leveraged the power of his stories, his family, and society and turned it back against largely white audiences. Further back, it is what sat in the lungs of enslaved Black people who created hymns that they sang openly in the presence of white people, communicating not only their pain but also their prayers and plans to escape. Black vibranium, this precious ore that's sat in the maw of our souls, has been the engine of constant change, dignity, defiance, love. It is the fuel that allows Michelle Obama to stand before a 2016 Democratic National Convention crowd and say, "When they go low, we go high," vehemently reappropriating the energy that had been directed against her and her family for the last eight years, attacks that ranged from birtherism to ape memes. It is Allen Iverson's ability to absorb hits on the basketball court and get back up. Blackness, and the love of our Blackness as a thing akin to vibranium, was a protest anthem song; Kendrick Lamar's "Alright" was sonic vibranium, tenderly taking the pain we were often feeling and turning it into a triumphant ode to our collective energy, healing, and forward motion. The notion of vibranium—a malleable, adaptable, absorbent substance—is a stand-in for all the things we admire about us. It has been the necessity to not only take what is given to us but also to redevelop a relationship with our world as things are taken from us, too.

It also means that it's a vital thing to protect. "Protect your energy," the notion of self-care, the idea of the interiority of Blackness, and what it means for our essence to be within our realm and reign have all been of ongoing importance to Black people. I am thinking about the essence, the inestimable presence, of *cool* that often comes with the experience and perception of Black culture. How that source of power, a coolness created at times in opposition to authority and oppression, and sometimes created in a beautiful Black vacuum unconcerned with anyone else, has been a lightning rod for interlopers to come in and seek to pillage this resource from us. If we were also willing to look at vibranium as this—the coolness, the powerfulness, the allure of Black culture—you can also see how, much like in the film itself, it is a material presence that's been routinely mined, reappropriated, and used and misused by others, often without knowledge of or care for its origin and meanings. The cross-armed stance of "Wakanda Forever," something that became both envy and energy, was as much a shield and a warning against those trying to get inside—consider how that formation is an "X" that says "do not pass"—as something that is endemic to Black America retaining its power, people, and pride.

I'm here to tell you that vibranium is real. How do I know it's real? Because I've sat in Black churches and felt the energy that wells up in there, sitting in the pews, our throats full of layered spiritual emotion. I've been to Howard Homecoming and seen the way we collectively coalesce into joy and music. That's vibranium. It's the chatter and change that happen in our beauty shops and barbershops, those community gathering places where we reconnect and remake ourselves. That's vibranium. It's in our inexhaustible ability to create new dance crazes, to take over social media platforms and create our own dialogues, personas, slang, and culture. Black people hum with the continual motion and energy that make vibranium vibrate; it is in the soles of our feet taking us on the Great Migration, and in the knees of our protest. That's vibranium. It's in our dirtbike street culture that's happening in Oakland, Baltimore, DC, Philadelphia. It's in the real way we quietly convene and find each other in the office and other cultural spaces, activating a channel of release with each other about what's happening to us and around us.

I know it is real because I've seen love, Black love, between our people; seen the transference of this power into the creation of family. Vibranium is in the naming of our children; it is in the lineage we create in our families. It is the energy that was passed between my Pop-Pop and me as we held hands during his last breaths in the hospital. Absorb, store, and release. Vibranium is in the loving way we collectively embrace ourselves. Vibranium may not be a real substance, but it has a real presence in our lives.

And I know it's real because of when I saw *Black Panther* on opening night while I was on vacation in Paris. We'd stood in line for over an hour in an uncharacteristically cold Paris winter with the type of array of Blackness that you could only find in a place like Paris. It was international in feeling, in scope, in strength. When the velvet rope and glass doors finally opened to let movie-goers in, we climbed the majestic theater steps and sat in a grand ballroom teeming with Black people. The entire room hummed in a way that I've only felt a few times before and after: walking Broad Street that morning the day after Obama won the presidency, and years later marching through downtown Philadelphia in unity and mourning during 2020's summer of reckoning. A large burgundy curtain covered the movie screen, and the din of excitement in the theater supercharged everyone in and out of their seats. We exploded and reexploded at several moments: when the curtains slowly opened to reveal the screen; when the Marvel opening logo ended and the voiceover began; when the credits finally ended as T'Challa stood before the world. The diasporic Blackness in the theater and the sheer joy in that room made me and many others in that space cry. Our tears likely meant a lot of things for a lot of people for a lot of reasons. But I know they were good tears. That's vibranium.

It's unlikely that Lee and Kirby knew what they were doing when they interlaced vibranium with T'Challa's origin story. An African king—a *Black man*—and his people in possession of the world's greatest resource? That in the heart of a fictional African country lay the promise of the future, the power of now? Given the tensions between Black people and the rest of the world, the focus on mining Wakanda for every ounce of its vibranium feels wildly familiar for peoples who are often fending off the notions and entreaties of appropriation. Vibranium as a resource, an enviable tool for exploitation, power, and wealth, is a wholly familiar tale that's still being written. The ability to absorb, store, and release this fantastic energy into the world is indeed the story of Black America—a group that has had to make sense and life out of the inhuman slave trade, the abnormality of the Jim Crow era, the insidiousness of the War on Drugs and its reptilian cousin, mass incarceration. Putting all those energies, experiences, joys, and hurts into social, political, and cultural language and action has been the way that Black America has continued to endure. Vibranium has been made real by our stories, our families, our triumphs, and our injustices. As we continue on now, years after both the film and Chadwick Boseman's life are over, the energy that both have given us has been absorbed, stored for another time, waiting for a beautiful release. This is proof that Wakanda is not only forever, but everywhere and enduring. That's real.

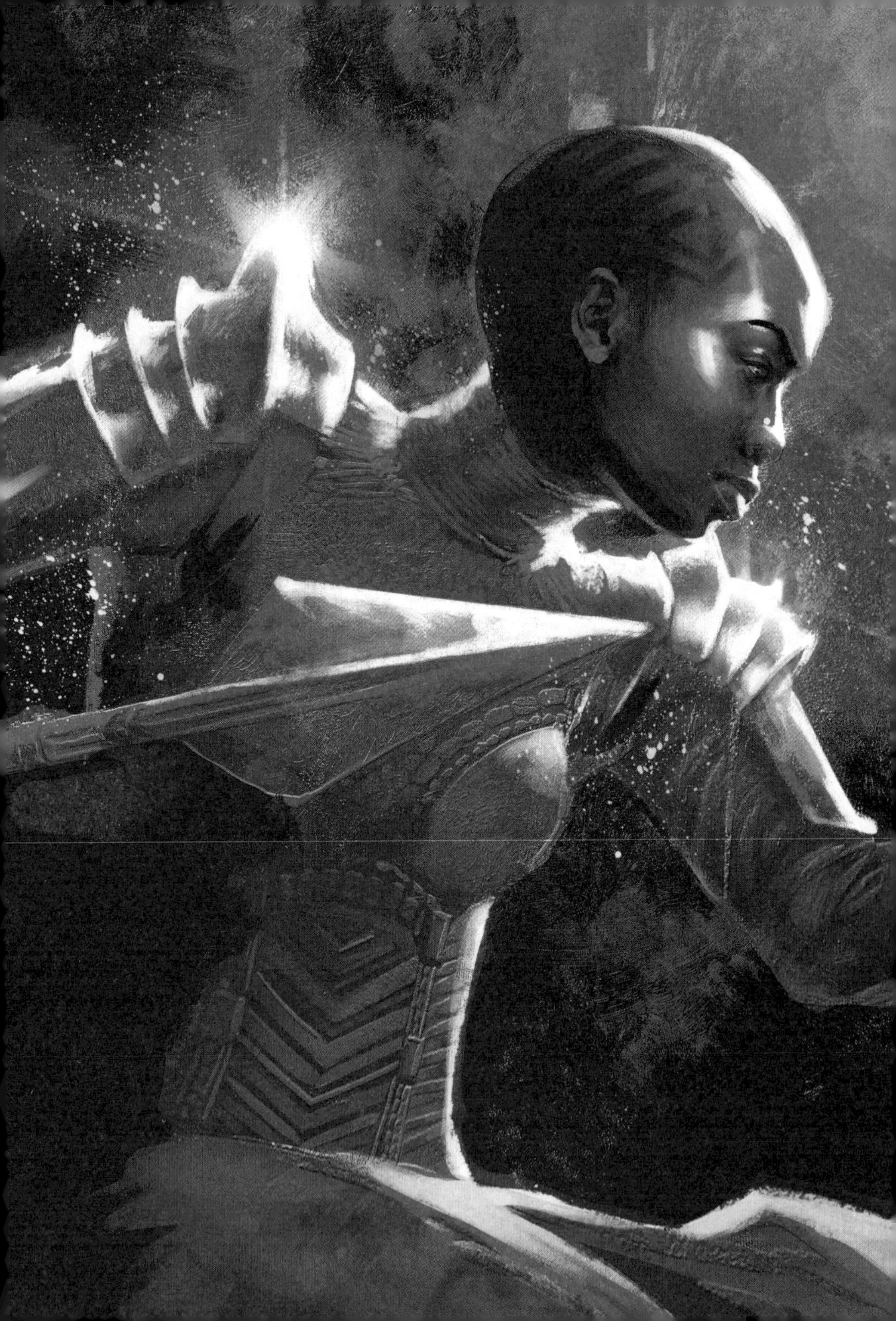

THE MUSIC OF
BLACK PANTHER

◇

Hannah Giorgis,
culture writer, *The Atlantic*

A BITTERSWEET VOICE SOUNDTRACKS some of the final moments of *Black Panther*. When T'Challa (played by the late Chadwick Boseman) and Shuri (Letitia Wright) step onto a basketball court in Oakland, thousands of miles away from the painful battles they've fought in Wakanda, audiences hear the quiet rumbling of a rapper born less than a hundred miles north.

Mozzy, the Sacramento-raised artist who appears twice in the film's official soundtrack, is at his best on "Sleep Walkin," the song that plays before T'Challa tells Shuri that they're standing outside the building where their father, King T'Chaka (John Kani), killed their uncle. "Sleep Walkin" is an eerie track, the kind that got under my skin within seconds of its first notes playing. If you're not familiar with some of the Northern California slang that populates its lyrics, you might miss just how mournful the song is. "Helped them n***** get them chains and showed the hood a different way" can sound like an aspirational goal at first blush, but Mozzy complicates any easy endorsements of

Black wealth. "Sleep Walkin" is as much a chronicle of all he's lost as it is a celebration of where the rapper is now, a depth of meaning that made the song immediately jump out to me when I heard it during my first *Black Panther* viewing of many.

Though it sounds like the perfect musical pairing for a film that traces the complex emotional landscape of the African diaspora through a super hero story, Mozzy himself wasn't always so sure that'd be the case. Back in 2018, several months after *Black Panther* premiered in the United States and just a few days ahead of the release of his album *Gangland Landlord*, I had the opportunity to interview Mozzy for *The Atlantic*. The rapper told me he hadn't been aware of how big a deal his inclusion on the soundtrack would be, much less how clearly "Sleep Walkin" would capture the tone—and heart—of the film. "My management tried to tell me the magnitude of it. I really didn't comprehend," he said. "But after the rollout and I seen that shit, I was like, *This is crazy*. So now I got a whole newfound respect, you feel me, for just the whole camp over there, the whole team."

The camp Mozzy referred to was Top Dawg Entertainment, or TDE, the label that fellow California rapper Kendrick Lamar worked with when he spearheaded the film's soundtrack. Kendrick's fingerprints are noticeable throughout the album, not just because the Compton artist features himself on it or because he drew from distinctly West Coast sounds when pulling it together. Like Mozzy, Kendrick excels at making music that conveys the melancholia and wonder of Black life—sometimes in equal measure, and other times with an explicit focus that nonetheless makes room for conflicting feelings.

Nowhere is that more evident than on *Black Panther: The*

Album, which caps Kendrick's oeuvre with grace and intentionality. The film's soundtrack builds on themes and musical flourishes present in the rapper's earlier works, projects I've been listening to since well before *Black Panther* drew connections between the California I knew and the Wakanda I'd discover onscreen. Take *Good Kid, M.A.A.D City,* his second studio album. Subtitled *A Short Film by Kendrick Lamar,* the album unfurls itself with cinematic precision and complexity. It opens with a prayer, then cuts to Kendrick sitting in his mother's van, headed to see a girl named Sherane. Listeners don't just get sounds; we get snapshots. Kendrick holding on to family; Kendrick processing grief; Kendrick willing himself into a more auspicious future. In those scenes, we catch glimpses of the seeds that would develop into Kendrick's later works—including the songs by artists he'd pick for the *Black Panther* soundtrack.

It's hard for me to listen to "Backseat Freestyle" now without recalling the hypnotic lyricism of Mozzy's "Sleep Walkin." On the *GKMC* track, Kendrick raps, "All my life I want money and power / Respect my mind or die from lead shower." That line could've been either morbid or flush with resentment. But on "Backseat Freestyle," and within the larger context of *GKMC,* it instead chronicles the artist's attempt to grow into a more potent version of himself. What separates it from more individualistic expressions of bravado is how intentionally *GKMC,* like the rest of Kendrick's repertoire, relays the experiences of other Black people—whether that's Kendrick's relatives, his friends, or those he grew up around in Compton. With its portrait of Kendrick's tumultuous but grounding relationship to his hometown, *GKMC* is as much a community record as it is a personal manifesto.

That same ethos, a style of musical arrangement that reflects the interconnectivity of Black people everywhere, not just in the same city, drives *Black Panther: The Album*. The soundtrack packs its forty-nine-minute runtime with songs from SZA, plus California heavyweights like Lamar and Mozzy; southern legends like 2 Chainz, Future, Travis Scott, and Swae Lee; the British R&B singer Jorja Smith and Ethiopian-Canadian crooner The Weeknd, as well as the South African artists Babes Wodumo, Saudi, Sjava, and Yugen Blakrok. The album vibrates with an impressive melange of genres—R&B, pop, soul, trap, and South African house among them. In that, it begins to reflect the starkly interconnected nature of Black music across the diaspora, including the ways that technology has rendered those linkages far more visible than ever before. "The movie's not set in 1910, or the 1960s when *Black Panther* first came out—it's set in today," the TDE producer Sounwave told NPR Music in 2018. "There's 'today' moments happening in the movie, so we want the whole soundtrack to sound like that too."

But the record also looks back in time, at least a little bit. On the official *Black Panther* soundtrack, you can hear echoes of the 2014 trip to South Africa that changed Lamar, which influenced the album that would become his landmark 2016 record, *To Pimp a Butterfly*. "I felt like I belonged in Africa. I saw all the things that I wasn't taught," Lamar told the writer Andreas Hale in an oral history of *To Pimp a Butterfly*, which the Recording Academy published ahead of the annual Grammy Awards at which *TPAB* was up for Album of the Year.

Speaking about that album was one of the first times Lamar had publicly discussed his relationship to the continent. It's not hard to see why working with Lamar on the sound for *Black Panther* was a no-brainer for director Ryan Coogler. "I've been a massive Kendrick fan ever since I first heard him, since his mixtapes, and I've been trying to track him down," Coogler said in that same 2018 NPR interview in which Sounwave laid out some of the soundtrack's production choices. When the *Black Panther* director finally did get to collaborate with Kendrick, after the rapper had finished working on his 2017 album *DAMN.*, Coogler was pleasantly surprised that Kendrick and his team went from working on "a few songs" to significantly upping their role. (It didn't hurt that by then, Kendrick and the others involved had seen several scenes from the unreleased film.)

Some of the soundtrack's standout tracks are the ones on which Kendrick appears, of course. When it plays during the film's credits, "All the Stars," Kendrick's collaboration with SZA, ends the theatrical experience with an electric, otherworldly crescendo. It made leaving feel nearly impossible, even if you don't already know about Marvel's post-credits scenes. Struck by the buoyant song, I remember wanting to sit right back down and experience the whole thing all over again.

On the album itself, the title track, "Black Panther," builds to a triumphant declaration of the Marvel hero's strength—and of Kendrick's. "King of my city, king of my country, king of my homeland / King of the filthy, king of the fallen, we living again," Kendrick raps with minimal production backing him. Again, the song conveys equal parts burden and blessing: "All hail the king, I dropped a million tears / I know several responsibilities put me here." The crown—Wakanda's, the rap game's—may glisten, but it's heavy, too.

But even so, the most refreshing, sonically interesting stretches of the soundtrack are those that explicitly emphasize ties across the diaspora. On "X," the South African rapper Saudi joins ScHoolboy Q and 2 Chainz, slipping between English and Zulu with addictive rhythm. "Imali is my Achilles heel, yeah / I race you to a hundred million," he raps, a reference to wealth very much in keeping with Wakandan splendor. Equal parts invigorating and soporific, "X" is a party track that would sound at home in any fete. And Babes Wodumo, the South African gqom artist and choreographer, lends gravity and depth to "Redemption," the uptempo banger she features on with the TDE singer Zacari.

Though Wakanda is a fictional East African nation, *Black Panther: The Album* doesn't feature much by way of music from real-life countries in that region. I'm reminded of what writer Lawrence Burney noted in a 2018 column for *Noisey*: "Regardless of whatever language barriers may exist, what typically unites black people worldwide on social media platforms is the music and accompanying dances being created throughout the diaspora." It's a missing piece I found myself longing for. Still, *Black Panther: The Album* represents a remarkable shift in what's possible for big-picture soundtracks, especially those helmed by the likes of Marvel. For a music nerd like me, that was—and still is—thrilling.

That Mozzy, a scrappy lyricist from Sacramento, could feature alongside Zulu-speaking stars like Sjava isn't something that would've seemed realistic at almost any juncture prior to *Black Panther*'s release—especially not on a song where Mozzy can rap lines like "Trapped in the system, traffickin' drugs / Modern-day

slavery, African thugs / We go to war for this African blood."
Being chosen for the soundtrack, and shouted out by Kendrick at
the Grammys, was an indelible experience for Mozzy. Those ges-
tures reminded him what's made Black music—and Black resistance more broadly—so special for so long. As he told me back
then, "It inspired me to go hard. Like I gotta get to bruh level, I
gotta get to that Kendrick Lamar level, I gotta get to them greats,
you know what I'm saying, so I can double back and I could do
that for somebody."

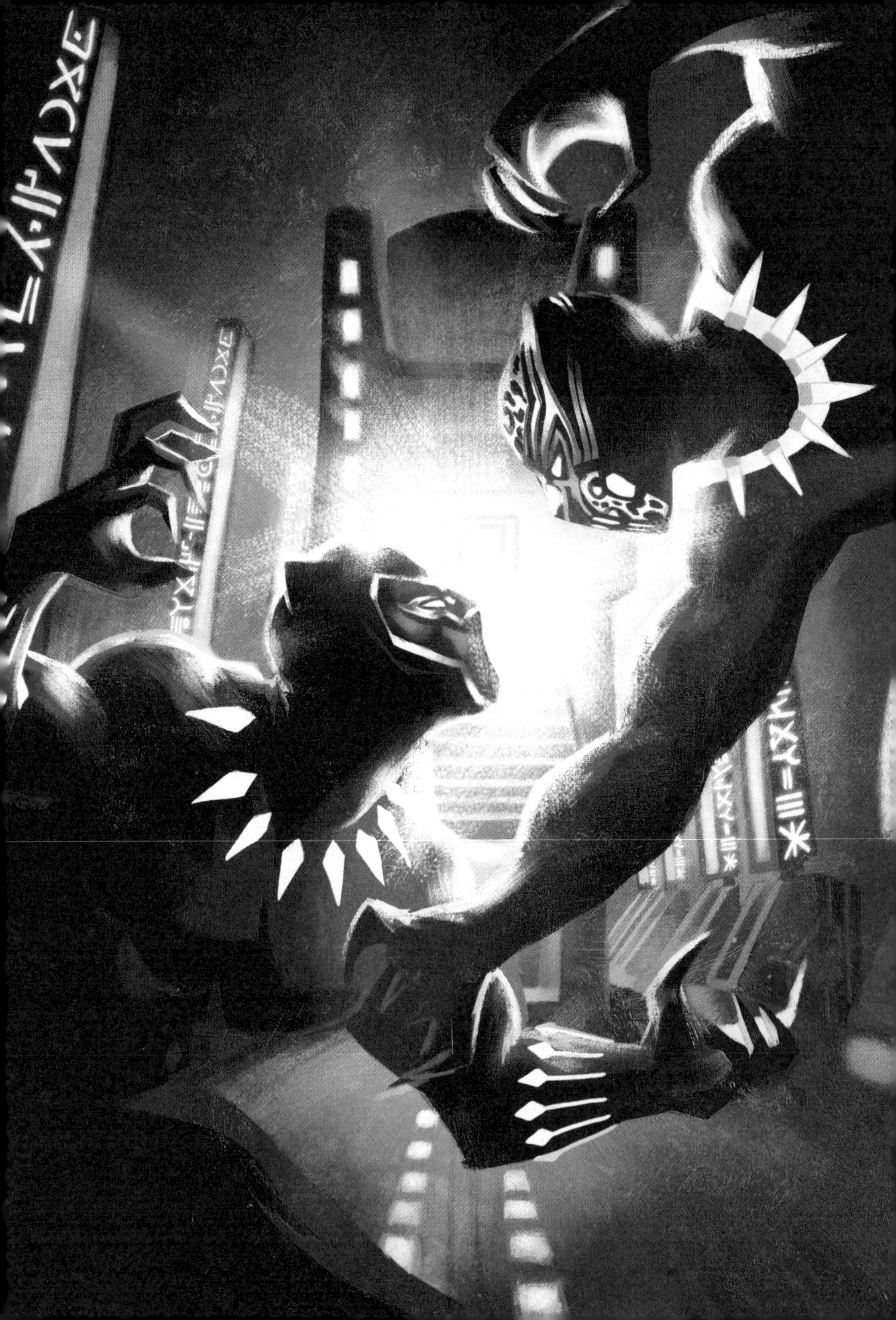

"THE T'CHALLA EFFECT"
AND ITS ENDURING INFLUENCE
ON POPULAR CULTURE

Gil Robertson IV, founder and CEO of
the African American Film Critics Association (AAFCA)

F EAR IS AN EMOTION that I have grown accustomed to feeling as a Black man, especially in the United States. As a Black man, I am used to knowing that every day I may face physical attacks just because of the color of my skin. For me the deaths of Emmett Till, Trayvon Martin, and George Floyd were not anomalies but, instead, fates that could easily befall me as well. It's an unspoken fear, one that is as silent as it is omnipresent. It is like a Sisyphean affair—just when you think you have it all worked out, things pop up that leave you with doubt. The strain on your mental health is immense and sometimes you feel like you're going to crash. If you're lucky, however, you keep moving forward, hoping for something to break all the pressure. Then, on top of it all, there are relentless waves of media messaging regularly challenging my humanity. It's against this landscape that the blockbuster movie *Black Panther* arrived.

Huge box office success aside, *Black Panther*'s impact extends far beyond its commercial milestones. For legions of Black men like me, the film challenged the popular assumptions associating us with only danger or trauma. *Black Panther* stemmed our fear, if only for a moment, by offering rare and complex portraits of Black manhood that are even more rare on the big screen. Audiences fell in love with the film's energy as they watched the beautiful citizens of Wakanda and their warrior king. Black men like me, along with the Black community at large, held on to this film so ferociously because, for us, *Black Panther* greatly surpassed a mere entertainment experience. It also validated us—made us feel seen and loved.

The big screen has long betrayed us with imagery and storylines that routinely devalue our humanity. From its earliest origins in the derogatory minstrel shows that served as its foundation to silent films like D. W. Griffith's toxic *Birth of a Nation* and the emergence of "talkies" like *Tarzan* and countless others, cinema has been hell-bent on obscuring who we are by co-signing and amplifying the systemic lies created around our mere presence.

My first memories of the movies started out fondly. Going with our family to drive-in theaters back in the early 1970s, my brother and I always felt super cool catching glimpses of popular films like *Shaft, Super Fly,* and *Cleopatra Jones*. As I grew older, however, I began to question those myopic depictions. Why did so many of these Black films fail to reflect and represent the variety of Black men and Black people that I knew in my own life? Nothing changed throughout my upbringing as Hollywood continued to serve up the same diet of Black movies that fell into three buckets—mindless comedies, hood stories, and the occasional "quality" project that was either rooted in slavery or revisited some other traumatic episode of Black life.

As I entered adult life, I began to understand cinema's power to influence and realized that it is a powerful tool for shaping how people see themselves as well as how they are viewed around the world. Unfortunately, the narrow portraits of Black men and Blackness overall promoted by the industry did little to favor us. Many of them created irreparable harm, damaging perceptions of Black men, of me. This is one of the many reasons *Black Panther*'s arrival felt so overdue. Instead of limiting us, its DNA reflected boundless possibilities, be it T'Challa; his father, T'Chaka; their advisor, Zuri; his best friend, W'Kabi; his compatriot and rival, M'Baku; or his challenger, Killmonger.

While much of the action or conflict in *Black Panther* revolves around T'Challa and Killmonger's battle for supremacy over Wakanda, the film gives space to these other Black men. Even though the scope of their character arcs may seem small, each of these Black male characters possesses endearing and relatable traits. Each has a purpose, which makes their storylines even more meaningful. But, as in real life, Killmonger commands the most attention. Perhaps that's because his rage is not just palpable but highly relatable. Like far too many of us, Killmonger is lost in an uncaring world, and while his actions don't deserve our sympathy, we understand where they come from. We understand that he is really looking for help in finding his way. He represents the fear that cripples and ultimately destroys far too many of us.

And then there's T'Challa, aka Black Panther, who is a ruler possessing the highest intellect and impeccable character. He accepts his responsibility to rule as Wakanda's king with a sense of purpose that I suspect has never been seen in any Hollywood movie about an African king. T'Challa is confident and unafraid to share some of his gifts and Wakanda's resources for the betterment of all of humankind. Portrayed in the movie with much grace and dignity by the late actor Chadwick Boseman, he delivered a hard-hitting uppercut to Hollywood's relentless volley of negative portrayals of Black men, bending the way in which Black men are framed in cinema hopefully forever.

From the very beginning, I knew that *Black Panther* was going to be a different kind of movie; I just didn't know how different. But I was sold the moment I realized that much of the film's action would center around the enormously wealthy and technologically advanced African nation of Wakanda. Not only was it game on, but *Black Panther,* overall, was that critical counterpunch to many of cinema's dismissive and undermining narratives on the status and worth of African people and their descendants.

Before *Black Panther,* Hollywood had largely positioned Africa as a forbidden place filled with dangerous jungles, savage natives, corrupt dictators, poor, sick, and starving people, or all of them at once. This cinematic positioning greatly damaged how the African continent has come to be viewed. That negative perception also created an attitude of shame for those of us of African descent about our place of origin. To my delight, *Black Panther* had none of that. It offered depictions of Africa that all could embrace, while making Black people and Black men look at our real Wakandas as proud places to call home.

In *Black Panther,* Black women were lauded not just for their beauty but also for their brains, wisdom, and warrior strength, with the Dora Milaje. Black men and women were not at odds and instead came together to protect what matters most—each other.

I'm not naive enough to believe that one film can obliterate Hollywood's century-long campaign of misinformation about Black men or Black people. But what I do know is that when I and other men like me look at this film, we see more of ourselves than we've ever seen before. And it's a good feeling. That fear I have always felt has not disappeared, but now it does keep company with hope. *Black Panther* isn't the complete answer, but it's an important start. It's raised the bar that will hopefully lead to others further expanding how Black men are presented on the big screen and seen throughout the world. And while that's not everything, it is a little bit more than we had before.

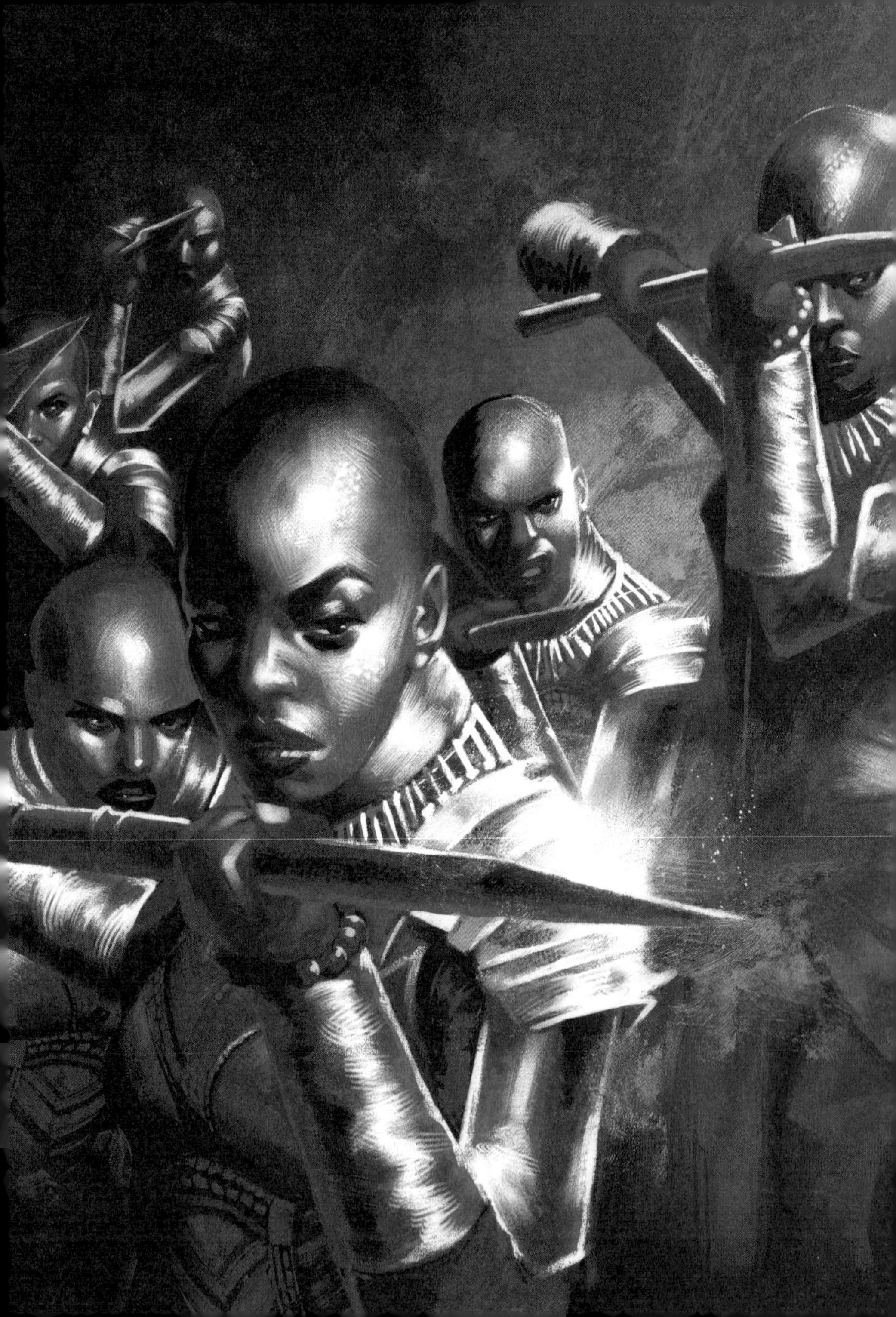

HIDING IN PLAIN SIGHT: *BLACK PANTHER*'S TREASURE TROVE OF PAN-AFRICAN HISTORY AND CULTURE

Marlene Allen Ahmed, associate professor
of English literature, United Arab Emirates University

WHEN *Black Panther* was released in 2018, the much-anticipated film received global acclaim for its portrayal of the African super hero and its depiction of the fictional, technologically advanced country of Wakanda. *Black Panther* is an impressive display of its creators' vision of the vibranium-fueled society built by the Wakandans and features a futuristic filmic atmosphere. Along with its avant-garde world, *Black Panther* also skillfully merges references to African and African American histories, cultures, and important leaders to show how its world and plot draw from the past. Thus, not only does *Black Panther* provide an entertaining cinematic experience for the viewer, but with its many allusions to the past, the film also offers fascinating insight into African history.

One of the most significant ways *Black Panther* references African history is by representing strong, fierce women. An example is the portrayal of the Dora Milaje, Wakanda's elite group of all-female warriors. These women are modeled on the Dahomey

Mothers (called Dahomey Amazons by European colonizers), the all-female military unit who served as the king's bodyguards in the seventeenth century before playing pivotal roles in Dahomey's fight against French colonization. These women fought alongside men and sometimes in the place of men when there were not enough men to fill the Dahomey military. They were accorded high status in Dahomeyan society. Through depictions of the Dora Milaje's fierce fighting skills, especially in the movie's climactic battle scene between those loyal to T'Challa and those who joined Erik "Killmonger" Stevens's coup d'état, the filmmakers of *Black Panther* honor the spirit of the Dahomey Mothers and the crucial roles they played in the Dahomey empire of the past.

Though African societies are typically thought of as being patriarchal, throughout history many women have played important leadership roles in their respective societies, similar to those played in the film. In the film, two of the elders in the Wakandan Tribal Council who represent the Mining Tribe and Merchant Tribe are women. Their presence on the council represents women who have historically held these roles, especially during Africans' prolonged fights against European enslavement and colonization. One such historical figure is Queen Ana Nzingha of Ndongo and Matamba, now the country of Angola. Queen Ana is still revered today in both Angola and Brazil, where many of her people were relocated after they were kidnapped and sold into slavery, because of her fierce efforts to defend her people. She did so through skilled diplomacy by learning Portuguese and being baptized as a Christian. She also formed an alliance between her people, the Ndongo, and the Portuguese in an attempt to keep the Portuguese from stealing her people and selling them into slavery. When the Portuguese broke their alliance, she and her people moved and settled in Matamba, where she instituted a new form of military organization called the *kilombo*. In this system, soldiers resided together in a fortified compound to defend themselves from the Portuguese. Through this practice, Ana was able to successfully defend her kingdom against Portuguese colonization for forty years. Her *kilombo* military strategy later was replicated in *quilombos* created in Brazil and other parts of Latin America by maroons. Maroons were slaves who escaped from the oppressive and abusive conditions of their enslavement and settled in mountainous or other remote areas to create their own independent living spaces. One of the most famous *quilombos,* Palmares, was a thriving community in the seventeenth century of over 30,000 people who defended themselves against the Portuguese using capoeira, a fighting style that has been given special status by UNESCO as a unique intangible heritage. Significantly, one of the fighting styles used by T'Challa in *Black Panther* is capoeira and represents people of African descent's historical resistance to enslavement and colonization. Wakanda, therefore, can be seen as a fictionalized *quilombo* as it, too, is a hidden powerful nation built by people of African descent who distanced themselves from the chaos of the outside world.

Black Panther's evocation of the history of Ethiopia is another way that it incorporates the theme of African resistance against slavery and oppression. This is most evident through the film's use of fidäl, an African alphabet that is used only for Ethiopian languages. In several transitional scenes in *Black Panther,* title cards are first presented in fidäl and then translated into

English. Furthermore, as Wakanda is presented as a country that has never been colonized, it bears similarities to Ethiopia. Ethiopia is renowned throughout the diaspora as the only African country that was never colonized. While Italy tried twice to colonize Ethiopia, the country was strong enough to defeat Italy in the Battle of Adwa of the First Italo-Ethiopian War in 1896 and the Second Italo-Ethiopian War from 1935 to 1937.* Ethiopia has also played a central role in creating the Organization of African Unity, an association established in 1963 whose vision was "the manifestation of the pan-African vision for an Africa that was united, free and in control of its own destiny."† Thus, Ethiopia historically played the role that Wakanda portrays in *Black Panther*'s fictional world, especially at the end of the film when T'Challa creates the Wakandan International Outreach Centre in Oakland, California.

Beyond bearing a striking resemblance to Ethiopia, the world of Wakanda also brings in aspects of other African cultures. For instance, throughout *Black Panther,* there are allusions to the Zulus of South Africa and their renowned leader Shaka Zulu. King T'Chaka's name itself is a reference to Shaka Zulu. Additionally, Queen Mother Ramonda's South African–style headdress is like the crown worn by Nandi, the mother of Shaka Zulu. Shaka Zulu, the founding father of the Zulu nation, is re-

---

* "First Italo-Ethiopian War," *New World Encyclopedia,* newworldencyclopedia.org/entry/First_Italo%E2%80%93Ethiopian _War.

† African Union, "About the African Union," au.int/en/overview.

vered for his impressive and revolutionary military tactics that made his nation a powerhouse in nineteenth-century southern Africa. Like Killmonger, Shaka Zulu grew up away from his father's kingdom and suffered the death of his mother, Nandi, which had a profound effect on his mental state. Shaka Zulu's influence on *Black Panther* is also reflected in the pivotal scene when Killmonger challenges T'Challa for the kingship of Wakanda. When Killmonger breaks his assegai spear to make it shorter, it then resembles a shorter spear called the iklwa, which Shaka Zulu invented as one of the military reforms that gave the Zulus a tactical advantage over their enemies. Moreover, the shields both Killmonger and T'Challa use in their battle are modeled on the Zulus' Nguni shields.

Though the film directly references aspects of African cultures, there are also moments where *Black Panther* merges African history, culture, and artistic traditions with the futuristic technologies present in the kingdom of Wakanda. This includes the use of kimoyo beads ("kimoyo" means "of the spirit" in Xhosa, one of the African languages used in the film), worn by the Wakandans. These small beads made of vibranium are worn around the Wakandans' wrists. Each bead performs a separate task—they are used as communication devices, to remotely pilot vehicles, and to heal, among other functions. Beads have historical and cultural significance in African cultures. Waist beads worn by women similarly communicated ideas and meanings about the wearer. They served as "a symbol and celebration of womanhood, sexuality, healing, spirituality . . . protection . . . and wealth, among other things . . . The meaning of the colors and different shapes of beads varies with every community and they can be thought of as visual dialects. Each bead, color, and shape relay a different message depending on the giver/receiver."[*] In the past, beads were even used as currency in the African-European slave trade; the film rewrites this story so that the beads are used in the service of Wakandan technoculture instead of as a means of its exploitation and oppression.

Another fascinating way that *Black Panther* uses African cultural history and artistry is through masks. Masks traditionally have been worn throughout history by Africans during rituals, celebrations, initiation ceremonies, and other events. The masks are viewed as physical representations of ancestors, spirits, or animals, and many believe that when a person puts on a mask, the individual transforms into the entity that the mask symbolizes. This idea is skillfully woven into *Black Panther,* for not only does T'Challa use his mask to disguise his identity, as most super heroes usually do, but his mask also shows how he embodies the animal spirit of the black panther. For instance, during his fight with M'Baku for the kingship of Wakanda, T'Challa wears a traditional black panther mask (instead of the more technologically advanced mask that is part of his super hero costume), while M'Baku wears a gorilla mask that is the totem of the Jabari tribe. Prior to this fight, T'Challa had been stripped of his superhuman powers, so when he wears the African black panther

---

[*] Rukariro Katsande, "The Importance of Beads and Beadwork in African Culture, Part III," *Wilderness Safaris,* November 25, 2014, wilderness-safaris.com/blog/posts/the-importance-of-beads-and-beadwork-in-african-culture-part-iii.

mask, he and M'Baku are undergoing the African-culture-based transformation of man into beast during their fight.

In addition to the transformative spiritual powers of African masks, the film pays homage to the artistic nature and value of these works as well. When Killmonger visits the Museum of Great Britain to steal the vibranium axe, he is approached by a white woman tour guide as he looks at a display case. The woman proceeds to tell him the origin stories of the items. She informs him that one of the masks he asks about, a re-creation of the Queen Mother Pendant Mask of Iyoba, was made by the Edo people of Benin in the sixteenth century. The mask is a reproduction of a real work that was commissioned by King Esigie of Benin to honor the beauty and strength of his mother, Queen Idia. One of a pair of masks, it is still currently housed in the British Museum in London, with the other located in the Metropolitan Museum in New York City. The Queen Mother Pendant Mask of Iyoba is just one example of how Africans used masks to honor ancestors and important members of their societies.

Later in this same scene, Killmonger informs the museum tour guide that the vibranium axe, which she falsely identifies as originating from the Fula people of Benin of the seventh century, was actually created in Wakanda and taken by British soldiers in Benin. This scene alludes to the story of the Benin Punitive Expedition of 1897, in which a British military force responded to an attack on an official named James Phillips and his trading expedition by Benin. In retaliation, the British government ordered the Oba's palace to be burned and confiscated all the Oba's treasures. The art was taken to London and sold, with much of it winding up in museums. While the Nigerian government has asked for its stolen artwork to be returned, as of this writing the United Kingdom has only agreed to "loan" Nigeria's own treasures to them. Killmonger's correction of the tour guide's story of the axe's origins addresses the injustice that is still ongoing as many African countries have yet to recover their priceless works of art.

In addition to incorporating African history, the history of African Americans' resistance to slavery, racism, and oppression is also recalled in several parts of *Black Panther*. The debilitating consequences of the African slave trade for the contemporary African American is a major theme in the film. This is primarily represented by scenes that reveal aspects of Killmonger's life and why he wishes to take over Wakanda in order to use the country's advanced technologies to free the oppressed peoples of the world from tyranny. The first time we meet Killmonger is when we see his father, N'Jobu, receiving an unplanned visit from his brother, T'Chaka, in Oakland, California, in the year 1992. We are meant to comprehend several aspects of African American history in this scene. First is the significance of 1992, the year of the Los Angeles riots after the verdict in the Rodney King case, when police officers were acquitted of charges of using excessive force when they beat King while arresting him during a traffic stop. The clothing that N'Jobu and Zuri are wearing references gangsta rap group NWA, whose infamous song "F*** Tha Police," from their debut album *Straight Outta Compton,* released in 1988, caused controversy because of its lyrics protesting police brutality and racial profiling. The song even drew the attention of the FBI and other law enforcement groups and contributed to tensions between African Americans and the police in the 1990s.

These tensions are still felt today, both in the United States and globally, as protests of police brutality against Black people have persisted.

Black Panther's popularity is a testament to the ingenuity and creativity of the film's creators. The film emphasizes how Black people have globally fought against enslavement, colonization, and other forms of oppression. Its many allusions to the histories, cultures, leaders, and artistry of people of African descent make it a rich, multifaceted, and fascinating viewing experience for the audience, and it will surely thrill generations to come.

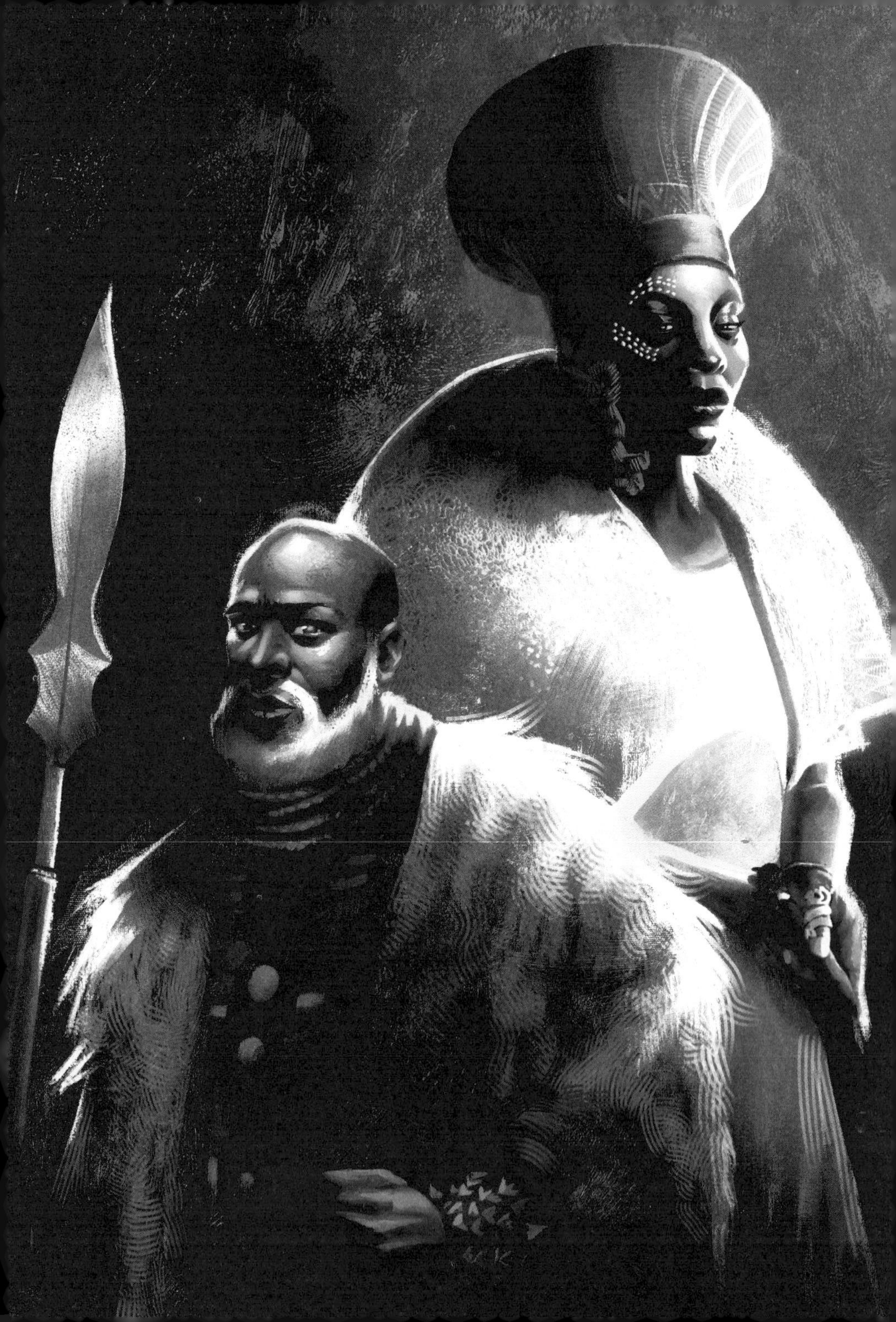

AFROFUTURISTIC BEAUTY:
THE COSTUMES OF *BLACK PANTHER*

◇

Ruth E. Carter, award-winning costume designer,
Black Panther and *Black Panther: Wakanda Forever*

MY WORK ON Marvel Studios' *Black Panther* has been a career-defining full-circle experience for me personally and as an artist. Two years after the 1964 Civil Rights Act, Stan Lee and Jack Kirby introduced Marvel's first Black super hero and the Afrofuturistic world of Wakanda into American culture. Half a century later, through costume design, thanks to Director Ryan Coogler, I had the incredible opportunity to bring this world to life.

When Marvel initially called, I thought, "Why me? I've never designed a super hero."

I was meeting with Producer Nate Moore and Ryan Coogler. I prepared for the interview with design concepts and sketches. I did a tremendous amount of research, including calling my concept artist friends who had childhood obsessions with comics.

When I arrived at Marvel Studios, it felt like I was entering the CIA, the way the doors locked behind me. My guest pass was like a retinal scan. During the meeting, I was getting anxious because I was having trouble bringing up images on Dropbox, but of course you cannot just log in to Marvel. You need to have an access code to get through their Tony Stark–like firewall. That was when Ryan said, "Ruth, I am so happy you are here."

I really cherish that moment. He made it feel like we had known each other our whole lives. I could feel the energy of a young Spike Lee pulsating through this man who had the vision to change the way Black people are perceived and received on-screen. I felt like I had auditioned to do the costumes for *Black Panther* when Ryan saw my work in *Malcolm X* as a young man with his father. From Ryan Coogler's perspective, I had been de-signing super heroes my whole life.

AFROFUTURISTIC DESIGN

To create the unique Wakandan looks and introduce new forms of beauty, I was inspired by the majesty of Africa and the ancestry of its tribes. By merging the traditional with the contemporary and incorporating technology to produce Afrofuturistic fashion and function, we came up with fresh ideas that empowered the female form and turned a super hero into an African king. I could sense we were changing the fabric of filmmaking.

CREATING THE BLACK PANTHER SUIT

The ideation and making of the Black Panther suit has been one of the most creative experiences of my life. Ryan Coogler's direction and vision are the driving forces behind the designs. Myself, Ryan, Marvel, an exceptionally talented group of concept artists led by Ryan Meinerding, and hardworking assistants created what is known as a "specialty costume design" for the Black Panther suit.

A specialty costume is an amalgamation of human, mind, and machine. It is a costume that has molded elements that are entirely created into a one-of-a-kind form. These unique elements are derived from computerized machines that compose physical materials from the design. Then specialty costume builders analyze every inch of the design—the direction of the stretch, the pattern, the way it wraps around the body—and make sure it will be exact per the costume design.

I immersed myself in learning the new language and process that went into building the super hero suit. We created a library of sample textures for the super hero suit and finally settled on one we called the Okavango triangle. We named this little triangle after the Okavango River that travels through Africa. The triangle is also considered a sacred geometry in Africa; its three points signify the mother, father, and child. This was very important to me. I wanted to make a strong connection between the Panther suit and Africa.

For some time, I observed the first Black Panther suit that was worn in Marvel Studios' *Captain America: Civil War*. It was displayed on a mannequin in my office, and I thought, "I should ask Chadwick Boseman to come to my office to try it on." That was one good way of getting that brilliant, fine actor in my office, but I really wanted to see him move and take on the suit. When the day came and Chad was dressed in the suit, it was complete and utter magic. As he put on the helmet, it became transformative. All of a sudden, I was like a kid—it felt like I was in the presence of a mythical being! Chad began to move around, assuming the dynamic poses of the Black Panther. I was beyond words. Though he looked amazing, I wanted to make sure his new suit gave him greater flexibility to perform to his highest ability, showcased how the use of vibranium, the strongest material in the universe, was connected with Wakanda, and, most importantly, reflected his taste as the Black Panther and king. The previous suit had been designed for his father, T'Chaka, but T'Challa's character was making a transformation from prince to king and bringing his own voice to the Black Panther. While reflecting on the making of the Panther suit, I realize how special a creative moment it was for me. It encompassed my journey in representing the culture. The suit is the epitome of Afrofuturism, defining our potential, not just in how we endured as a people but also in how we could have lived as Africans. It was significant to me and to the film that this new iteration of the suit showcased Wakanda's technological advances while being grounded in its African roots.

I learned the term "muscle sculpt" on this journey toward building the perfect super hero suit. (And no, it was not our nickname for either Chadwick Boseman or Michael B. Jordan.) We developed a muscle sculpt for the understructure of the suit, which was accomplished by creating a vacuum form (a mannequin) of Chadwick Boseman's body and then, with clay, sculpting more dynamic muscle shapes on top of his muscles. Ryan Coogler did not want Chad's sculpt to go too far into super hero form, so we developed the perfect proportions and then made a muscle suit to match. Since the suit is made of vibranium, it was my decision to allow the silver muscles to be seen underneath the top layer of the suit. We covered the muscles with a suit made from the thinnest Eurojersey and printed it with our Okavango pattern. There was a second pattern that was printed as well, a medallion in the center of the chest that had abstract lines that traveled around the suit. These lines would light up purple when the Black Panther met with kinetic energy. Together, the lines and the patterns created a Wakandan design that made the connection I was looking for between the suit and Africa.

T'CHALLA

Our king was channeled by the one and only, the late great Chadwick Boseman. Chad brought a heart of gold to the role of King T'Challa. It was very important to me to ensure he looked regal and majestic in his everyday attire. He wears several different hand-embroidered Nigerian senator suits that include a stylish tunic over smart trousers.

When the Black Panther/T'Challa arrives in Wakanda after his mission to rescue Nakia, portrayed by the sensational Lupita Nyong'o, he is flanked by her and General Okoye, captured perfectly by the impressively powerful Danai Gurira. The king is greeted on the landing pad by the queen mother, embodied by my longtime collaborator over six films, the legendary Angela Bassett. The queen has on one side her daughter, Princess Shuri, brought to life by rising star Letitia Wright, and on the other side is the second-in-command after the general, Ayo, played by the beautifully enchanting Florence Kasumba.

First impressions are key. In this opening scene, introducing these characters, we wanted to establish new forms of beauty and show how much of Africa is represented in the story and throughout the film.

QUEEN RAMONDA

We first see the queen mother's African royalty with her isicholo, a married woman's headdress of South African origin. When I researched this piece, I saw a crown. I wanted it perfectly shaped to look regal, and in order to do that, we had Queen Ramonda's isicholo crowns 3D printed. This also included her detailed shoulder mantle, which is patterned with African lace. These were 3D printed on flexible material so Angela Bassett could take them on and off, as they were essentially wearable art.

SHURI

Shuri, our genius tech prodigy, establishes a youthful Afrofuturistic look that is both functional and fashionable. She is wearing a West African adinkra symbol, traditionally worn by royalty, conveying purpose and perseverance—two things Shuri definitely possesses. Her royalty is also represented in the neckpiece with cowry shells symbolizing trade, wealth, and commerce among African tribes. Shuri's looks throughout the film are meant to both inspire and feel relatable, as if anyone could wear them.

THE DORA MILAJE: OKOYE AND AYO

The Dora Milaje costume is a fan favorite. When we first see Okoye, we are in awe, as we have seen and experienced nothing like this costume before. We take in her beauty and feel the power of her presence. Charged with protecting the king, Okoye leads the fiercest, highest-ranking female warriors in Wakanda. Within the Marvel Cinematic Universe, people know not to get tangled up with the Dora Milaje.

My first challenge with the costume was the long-front tabard, a vertical garment serving as an armor piece. Okoye's is beaded in the front. It started as a simple chevron down the front of the body. I wanted it to have a special reason for being African and to look like it was passed down to each wearer. If the tabard was going to be so prominent on this warrior costume, I needed it to be there for a good reason. African beads are symbols of social status and used extensively in art and sacred ceremonies to appeal to the spirits. So, with "protection" and "royalty" in mind, I beaded the entire tabard in the tradition of Nigerian Yoruba diviners' belts and added something special for each wearer toward the bottom of the tabard that signifies which tribe that Dora hails from, whether it was a crystal, a piece of jade, or a symbolic animal.

To show her rank as general, Okoye is wearing gold armor. Ryan Coogler wanted the armor on the Dora Milaje to look like jewelry, so we made sure that it had a real shine to it. They are also wearing neck and arm rings inspired by the South African Ndebele people. Ayo is seen wearing silver armor, as she is second in rank to the general.

The harness portion of the Dora Milaje costume around the bust represents the beauty of scarification in African culture. As it is a great honor to be a Dora Milaje, we wanted it to appear hand-tooled, as if the same craftsperson in Wakanda who makes the queen's mantle would be making the harnesses for the Dora Milaje. The beadwork is inspired by the Turkana people and the red color by the warriors of the Maasai, both of Kenya.

Ryan Coogler was very intentional about elevating the look of the Dora Milaje compared to some comics, where they are in overly sexualized uniforms. His vision did not include them wearing high heels, so we put them in split-toe boots. He wanted the uniform to be commanding yet empowering their feminine form. He wanted people to be enamored with their beauty and respectful of their power. We fully represented Africa in the Dora Milaje costume with its armor, bodice, tabard, scarification, tattoos, and adornments. This costume and the women who wear them have allowed people to see strength as beauty.

NAKIA

Nakia represents the River Tribe and has many roles as a spy, War Dog, challenger, and T'Challa's love interest. In the opening scene of the film, she is undercover as a spy observing trouble being made for defenseless women and children. We had her in a Nigerian burka, with her spy look underneath, and adorned her with a River Tribe stone. Throughout the film, you will see Nakia maintains a green palette, whether she is in her River Tribe challenge day attire or in the casino scene, where she stuns going undercover as a wealthy broker.

WARRIOR FALLS AND THE TRIBES

Ryan Coogler was very specific about many things, especially in the Warrior Falls scene. It was the one opportunity for all the Wakandan tribes to come together in their tribes' traditional garb—he needed it to be magnificent. He said that when we look up at that mountain, "we want it to be a feast for the eyes."

I was very excited to implement what I knew of the ancient indigenous people and tribes of Africa. We created unique looks for the different tribes of Wakanda: the Royal Family, Border, Merchant, River, Mining, and Jabari. I divided the costumes in the stockroom by color and assessed what was needed for each tribe. I had illustrations done to modernize some of the tribal looks to make them come alive, and then we began to build them. We also made more traditional pieces, like the beautiful light blue tops worn by Tuareg women, who reside in much of the Sahara region.

The fitting process was arranged around my schedule. I had to put my stamp on this entire moment—I had done so much research and I knew what looked the best for each tribe. As the North Africans have a distinctly different physical appearance from West Africans, I did not want to mess it up. So, in the fittings, I wrapped every turban, draped every elder, and made sure the proper beading was used for each tribe. I did not want to leave it to chance. The trick was getting people out of my brilliant concoctions and hanging them up as perfectly as possible so they could be redone on camera day. It was incredible getting everyone dressed for the Warrior Falls. I was proud to walk on set and see all the magic unfold.

ZURI

Zuri is the spiritual leader of Wakanda. He oversees the other priests and the cultivation of the Heart-Shaped Herb, as it gives the Black Panther access to his powers. He represents all the tribes of Wakanda, and so his look has much of Africa within it.

Like Nigerian men, he wears these big open-shaped garments. You also see beading along the front of his tabard in the tradition of the Turkana people. Zuri's poncho is made of tiny silk tubes sewn together to drop along his back, so when he stands in the water and turns, they blow and billow and have this magical effect. The triangular details on Zuri's sleeve are inspired by the Tuareg, as is the beautiful aubergine color with black and silver. In Wakanda, royal violet is the signature color of the priests and caretakers of the Heart-Shaped Herb.

MERCHANT TRIBE

The Merchant Tribe, based on the beauty of the Tuareg people of North and West Africa, represents the economic commerce of Wakanda. The elder, portrayed by the legendary Dorothy Steel, has these gigantic golden earrings worn in all their glory. They signify the enormous capital wealth available to Wakanda. She has Ethiopian-style crosses along the front of her drape, and her turban is adorned with the same Tuareg symbols. You can see more of this drapery-style wear on the other people of the tribe, who are standing behind the elder.

Standing next to the Merchant Tribe elder is her fierce warrior. He is adorned in the same African style of the Tuareg, with some crosses and symbols, as well as having his face covered, as is traditional for the men.

BORDER TRIBE

Ryan Coogler was inspired by the blankets of the Sotho people in Lesotho on his travels to South Africa and wanted them incorporated into the film. The Border Tribe elder M'Kathu, played by Danny Sapani, is wearing his heart-shaped headdress and is adorned with a blanket. We added the vibranium to the blankets by printing silver Wakandan language and designs on top. With the vibranium, they are able to defend themselves and shield their tools and weapons with their blankets, in addition to keeping themselves warm during colder weather.

W'Kabi, the Border Tribe warrior played by the incomparable Daniel Kaluuya, has Wakandan symbols on his blanket. Later in the film, when the tribes battle, we can see how the blankets turn into shields of vibranium for protection.

RIVER TRIBE

Nakia is wearing the costume of the top warrior of the River Tribe, which is inspired by the Suri or Surma people of southwestern Ethiopia. The people of the River Tribe care for the waterways and you see families along the rivers of different areas of Africa with children. They adorn their bodies with sticks and flowers, worshipping the wealth the river can provide. Nakia has her warrior harness complete with cowry shells that signify her great wealth.

The River Tribe elder, played by Isaach De Bankolé, wore a lip plate, which also signifies his status and wealth. His costume is completely beaded from African artifacts I found at flea markets. We then made his warrior-style kaftan with a drape and covered it with cowry shells and beadwork. The lip plate is completely prosthetic, and it took the makeup department hours to put on every day. The gauges in his ears are painted with the design work that you will see in some of his other costumes. That day on set he had to drink his beverages from a straw, but he still had the ability to hold a conversation.

MINING TRIBE

Responsible for mining vibranium, the Mining Tribe has a commanding presence. The elder portrayed by Connie Chiume is wearing a Himba wig, inspired by the indigenous people of northern Namibia, complete with little puffs on the bottom. This wonderful piece is made of an aromatic, shea-butter-like paste, and red clay from the earth to get the pigment. These elaborate hairstyles can reflect status, wealth, and rank. I drew the inspiration for the elder's amber crown from Alex Haley's *Roots*, the reboot of the miniseries. I brought it on because it framed her face so beautifully.

The Mining Tribe warrior is wearing a Maasai headdress. Worn by Maasai warriors of Kenya and Tanzania, the bigger the feathers or the fur that goes around the headdress, the more fierce the warrior. The beadwork around the face is usually done by hand by craftspeople, but this one happened to be done by me late at night in the costume shop because I was insistent on having the headdress in the Warrior Falls scene. The drapes on the body are long pieces of fabric that are knotted on the shoulder in a free-form creative process on the day we shoot.

SHURI AT WARRIOR FALLS

In the scene at Warrior Falls, Shuri is wearing her traditional costume to represent that she is a warrior. A beaded and boned prosthetic jaw of a panther is on her chin, which Letitia jokingly called "little MC underbite." It was made from special real African beads, some of them of clay and others of rolled paper. The corset was inspired by the Dinka people of South Sudan, and it travels around Shuri's body and attaches in the front. We wanted her to have all of this beading on her face and around her shoulders and body so she would appear royal, but it was super uncomfortable. It really did inspire her lines. When she turns slightly you can see the Dinka corset and the weight of the spear that goes up her back. It is the most incredible of costumes to wear at the Warrior Falls ceremony. If she had challenged her brother, T'Challa, in that costume, she probably would have taken a bite out of him.

JABARI TRIBE

Living in the mountains of Wakanda, the Jabari worship the White Ape and the gorilla god, Hanuman. They scowl at the use of vibranium and instead rely more on the strength of tempered wood and leather to meet the demands of their cold, mountainous region. The look for M'Baku, characterized by the charming Winston Duke, is inspired by the Dogon people of central Mali, West Africa. Ryan Coogler fell in love with the grass skirt look for the Jabari. I went in search of inspiration and found a grass piece with a strong manly tone at the Metropolitan Museum of Art in New York. The Dogon use pink and green colors, but since the Jabari reside in snow, I used rock and earth tones and put a leather sheath underneath the skirt and fur draping over their backs.

ERIK "KILLMONGER" STEVENS

Our complicated, seductive villain, Killmonger, is delivered to us by the ever so wonderful Michael B. Jordan. Killmonger is an outsider in his homeland. He is an African American guy raised in Oakland, California. His vibe is very American and unapologetic. I think Ryan Coogler felt that this character would spend twenty-five hundred dollars on a pair of Christian Dior combat boots. In the museum, we see Killmonger in a beautiful super-soft denim jacket lined with shearling that costs four or five thousand dollars. It had the right hang on him and speaks to American pop culture.

For this character, I had to take Michael B. Jordan shopping. I did not do this with anybody except him because everyone else was playing a Wakandan. He was the outsider American and we needed his costume to represent that.

A FULL-CIRCLE MOMENT

We made over a thousand costumes with five concept artists, three assistant costume designers, specialty costume companies, agers/dyers, mold makers, set costumers, and jewelry craftspeople to honor the beauty and history of Africa and the Dinka, Dogon, Himba, Lesotho, Maasai, Ndebele, Suri, Surma, Tuareg, Turkana, Wagenya, and Zulu peoples. The final product is Wakandan Afrofuturistic looks that have expanded our vision of beauty.

My life's passion and work is about telling diverse stories through costume design. Before a word of dialogue is uttered, costumes begin to tell the story of a character—who they are and where they have been. It is a visual narrative using fabrics, colors, and patterns that bring to life characters, whether they are real, historical, or imaginative.

My journey into this profession began when I was a girl growing up in Springfield, Massachusetts. The youngest of eight siblings, I relied on everyone in our home to entertain me. My brother was the artist, and I was incredibly inspired to be like him. I spent hours in my room at my desk being creative, whether it was drawing, coloring, or reading poetry and literature. One afternoon, I serendipitously discovered a sewing machine tucked inside the desk. My creative playground expanded. With the most modest of beginnings, this girl who knew how to dream, and pursue that dream by any means necessary, began building her love for creating art.

I nurtured my artistic curiosity over the years, and it led me to follow my family legacy at Hampton University, a historically Black college on the shores of Virginia.

Hampton is where the first freed enslaved persons and indigenous people were educated under the giant tree on campus, known as the Emancipation Oak. It is also where the Emancipation Proclamation was read aloud. It was here that the stories I read and learned connected me to who I was and where I came from. It lit up in me a passion to share these and other stories yet to be discovered and because of it, I enjoyed being in the theater department. I was drawn to it like a calling. This is where I discovered all my talents as an artist merged, and I found myself the costume designer on campus.

Coming up with the costumes for *Black Panther* was a full-circle life moment for me, personally. I think back to the moment I discovered the sewing machine. It was not unique to just our household; this was a common appliance in Black family homes. It was a staple, just like an iron. It connects me to my ancestors, who arrived in shiploads on these shores from Africa, vulnerable and naked, and had to learn to make clothes. From picking cotton all day in the heat to sewing, cutting, and dyeing, they were making clothes for themselves to maintain their dignity. Some became artisans behind closed doors, never earning the credit for creating such couture fashions for their owner, owner's wife, or employer.

That sewing machine I discovered was a direct connection to this legacy. To be able to use the same skills that my ancestors perfected to survive in order to tell the stories that give names to the nameless, elevate us, and allow us to understand ourselves better, has given me more understanding of a purpose I achieve every day.

To be recognized for designing costumes for Black characters living in all their glory without knowing colonization is a full-circle moment for me as an artist. I cherish knowing that my ancestors led me here. Seeing Ryan Coogler's vision through and adding my own signature to designing Afrofuturistic looks where people can find their own beauty represented is the greatest gift of my art. Giving new generations the confidence these characters carry by seeing a part of themselves on-screen. With that power, I hope they have the ability to live their purpose and manifest their own freedom in the vision of their futures.

THE OSCAR

When I think about hearing my name announced as the winner of the 2019 Academy Award for Best Costume Design for *Black Panther,* I still feel this incredible sensation of wonderment and awe!

My first Oscar by way of costume design felt like each moment in each chapter of my life allowed me to explore more deeply who I was as an individual, where I belonged in a culture, and where I am from in connection with my ancestors.

As I am walking up to receive the statue, I can see Chadwick Boseman, in the first row center, leap to his feet, throwing both arms in the air and waving them up and down as if to say, "We are not worthy." The joyful cheer that erupted from his soul rippled through the Dolby Theater, and it was a gift and blessing in itself seeing him react as if his favorite team had won. He led the standing ovation of a lifetime. I felt so valued as a person and as an artist by my peers. Chadwick Boseman and I previously worked on the film *Marshall* as well. We both have in common the business of bringing super heroes to life. He is dearly missed.

I didn't want to be just any costume designer; I wanted to be the best at my craft. I wanted to honor the heritage that was instilled within me. When I heard the roar of the crowd continue, I felt like every day I had showed up to work and all the Christmases and holidays I sacrificed, from my days in college to that Oscar moment, was worth it all.

Over twelve Spike Lee joints, especially on *Malcolm X,* Spike would say to me, "Don't think about the Oscar. Just channel your work to uplift the race."

That night, receiving my Oscar in Spike's presence and being able to thank him personally was something written in the stars.

Since the release of *Black Panther* and my win, scores of people—colleagues, fans, universities, colleges, groups, and organizations—have asked me how we came up with the costumes for Wakanda. When I feel audiences hooked on every word of my speeches, or see people creating their own Dora Milaje costumes or young girls dressed as Shuri, I can feel my purpose realized, as they see themselves to be strong, intelligent, empowered, and worthy of greatness.

> *Spike Lee, thank you for my start. I hope this makes you proud.*
>
> *Marvel may have created the first Black super hero, but through costume design, we turned him into an African king!*
>
> *It's been my life's honor to create costumes.*
>
> *Thank you to the Academy. Thank you for honoring African royalty and the empowered way women can look and lead on-screen.*
>
> *Thank you to my crews around the world who helped bring Wakanda to life.*
>
> *Our genius director, Ryan Coogler. You are a guiding*

force. Thank you for your trust and understanding my role in telling the African American story.

Adding vibranium to costumes is very expensive, so thank you, Victoria Alonzo, Kevin Feige, Luis D'Esposito, Jeffrey Chernov, Bob Iger, and Nate Moore.

My career is built with a passion to tell stories that allow us to know ourselves better.

This is for my ninety-seven-year-old mother watching at home. Mom, thank you for teaching me about people and their stories.

You are the original super hero!

—RUTH E. CARTER
2019 Academy Award for Best Costume Design
acceptance speech

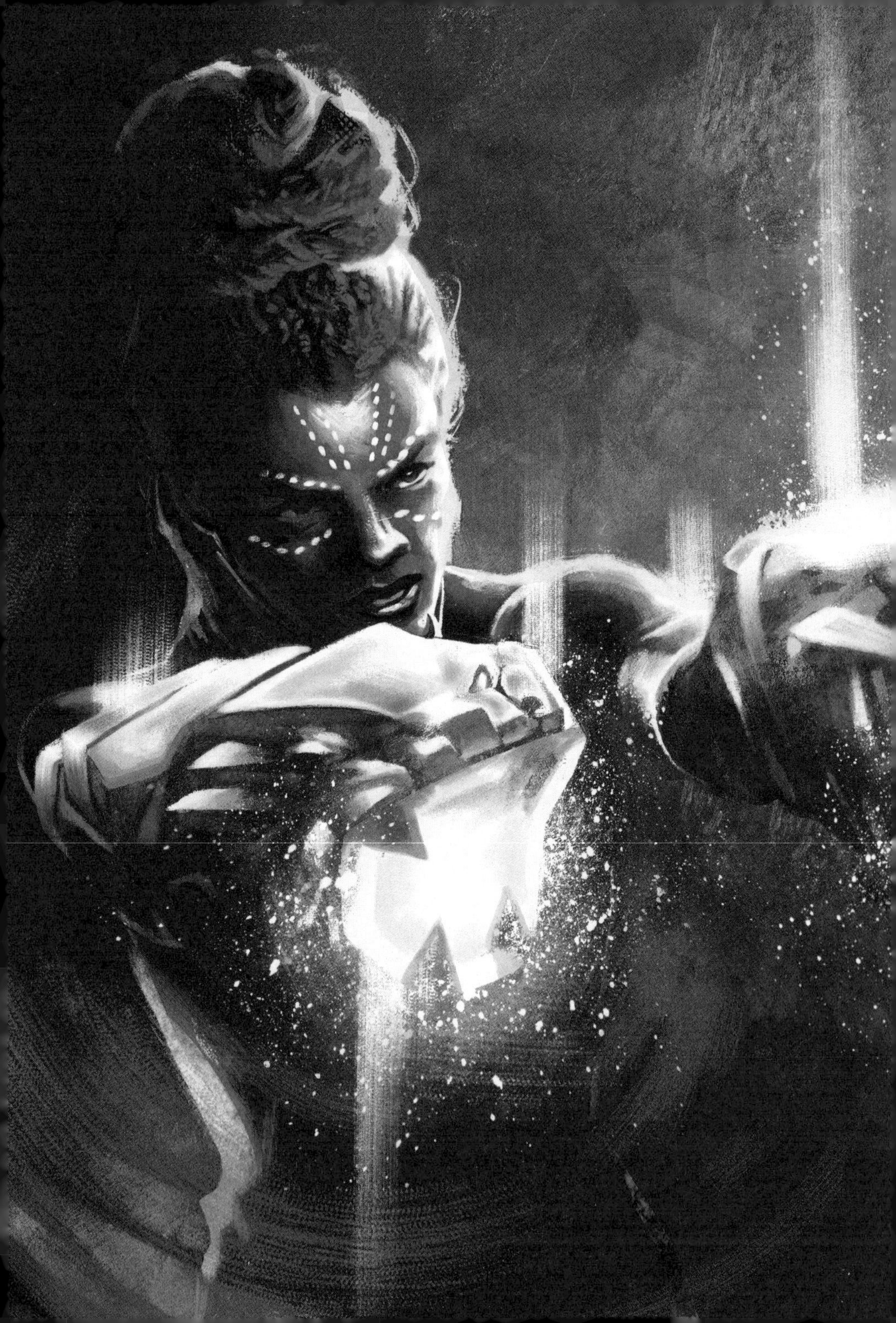

WAKANDA: A VISION OF
AFRICA'S PAST AND FUTURE

Dwayne Wong Omowale,
Pan-African activist and author

FOR MANY YEARS the portrayal of Africa in the West was largely negative. It has often been portrayed as a land of primitive savages and cannibals who lived in jungles. These negative portrayals of Africa were often used to justify Western racism against African people by depicting slavery and colonization as benefits for Africans because it introduced them to the superior civilization of Western cultures. Even after the decolonization of Africa, negative portrayals of Africa have continued to persist in the Western media. Civil war, child soldiers, pirates, disease, poverty, and famine are just some aspects of Africa that continue to predominate in Western portrayals of Africa. It is not that these issues do not exist in Africa, but that these negative portrayals reinforce the racist notion that Africans are incapable of developing and managing independent societies of their own. *Black Panther*'s portrayal of Wakanda challenges many of the prevailing Western stereotypes about Africa by presenting an African nation that is not only technologically advanced but deeply rooted in traditional African culture, political organization, and religion.

Unlike other African nations, Wakanda managed to avoid the adverse impacts of the slave trade and colonialism. In the opening scene of *Black Panther*, N'Jobu narrates to his son N'Jadaka (who later becomes the villain Killmonger) that Wakanda thrived for many centuries as conflicts and wars took place around the rest of the world. This scene shows a group of people who are chained together and being led toward a ship. This is a depiction of the Atlantic slave trade in which millions of Africans were stolen from Africa and dispersed throughout the Americas, where they were enslaved. This scene demonstrates that as the African continent endured being ravaged for centuries, Wakanda managed to stay hidden and safe.

To effectively protect itself from the chaos of the outside world, Wakanda exploited Western perceptions of African nations by outwardly presenting itself as an impoverished nation. The rest of the world had no reason to question this deception because Wakanda seemed just as impoverished and underdeveloped as neighboring African countries. What does seem to attract the curiosity of international observers is that despite this apparent poverty, Wakanda rejects foreign aid. Of course, this is before the rest of the world comes to find out that Wakanda is actually a very wealthy and technologically advanced nation. In fact, in the Marvel Cinematic Universe, Wakanda is the most technologically advanced nation in the world. This is due to the presence of a resource known as vibranium, which gave Wakanda the power to develop itself.

In 2021, Disney+ launched a series titled *What If . . . ?*, which presented alternative versions of events in the Marvel Universe. Wakanda presents a what-if scenario in the real world: What if Africa had never been colonized? What if African nations were free to utilize their own resources for their own development?

In 1884, THE DOMINANT POWERS of Europe came together at the Berlin Conference and divided Africa up among themselves. One by one, nations in Africa came under the domination of the colonial powers in Europe. The only two nations to escape being colonized were Liberia and Ethiopia. Liberia remained independent politically, but the United States exerted so much control and influence over Liberia that Liberia was a virtual colony of the United States. As a result of this scramble to colonize Africa, the African continent found itself under the political domination of foreign powers.

Colonial rule in Africa was often very brutal. One of the worst examples of this was in Congo, where it is estimated that more than 10 million Africans were killed as a result of Belgian colonialism. Apart from its brutality, colonial rule also underdeveloped Africa. The colonial powers exploited Africa's resources for their own benefit. This was often done at the expense of Africans who labored for the colonial governments but received none of the benefits from their work.

One of the justifications for the colonization of Africa was this notion that Africans were uncivilized. Of course, European colonizers defined civilization based on the standards of European societies. For this reason, the civilizing mission the Europeans engaged in was aimed at transforming the culture of Africa.

Africans were encouraged to adopt European culture to become "more civilized." In the French colonies, Africans who had assimilated into French culture were known as *évolué,* whereas in the Portuguese colonies such Africans were known as *assimilado.* This civilizing mission served the purpose of colonial subjugation by making Africans believe that being conquered and colonized by Europeans was a benefit for which they should be grateful.

To understand what Africa could have been without the adverse impact of colonialism, it is important to understand what Africa achieved prior to colonialism. Contrary to the way that the colonizers portrayed it, Africa was not a land of ignorant savages who were incapable of building civilizations on their own. One outstanding example of development in Africa is its architecture. Perhaps the most famous example of this is the monuments of Egypt, particularly the Great Sphinx and the pyramids. The civilization of Kush, which was located to the south of Egypt, built pyramids as well. Kush built more pyramids than the Egyptians did, although the Kushite pyramids were much smaller than the Egyptian pyramids. In Ethiopia, there are impressive monuments, such as obelisks constructed by the kingdom of Axum and churches at Lalibela that were carved out of rock. There are also the Walls of Benin in Nigeria, which protected Benin City. The 1974 edition of the *Guinness Book of Records* described the Walls of Benin City as the world's largest earthworks carried out prior to the mechanical era.

Metallurgy also existed throughout Africa as early as 3000 B.C.E. Anthropologist Franz Boas suggested that Africans were smelting iron at a time when Europeans were still using stone tools. He wrote: "It seems likely that at a time when the European was still satisfied with rude stone tools, the African had invented or adopted the art of smelting iron. Consider for a moment what this invention has meant for the advance of the human race. As long as the hammer, knife, saw, drill, the spade, and the hoe had to be chipped out of stone or had to be made of shell or hard wood, effective industrial work was not impossible, but difficult. A great progress was made when copper found in large nuggets was hammered out into tools and later on shaped by melting, and when bronze was introduced; but the true advancement of industrial life did not begin until the hard iron was discovered."* Africans also developed an advanced method for producing steel. In 1978, two researchers named Peter Schmidt and D. H. Avery discovered that in Tanzania the Haya people were producing steel using methods that dated back 1,500 years. This method of producing steel involved using preheated blowpipes that were extended into the furnace chamber. This preheating method was not used industrially in Europe until the mid-nineteenth century.

African drums also display the ingenuity and creativity of African societies. Drums were not only used for music. In several different societies throughout Africa, drums were used as a means of communicating over long distances. Robert Campbell, a Jamaican man who traveled to West Africa, provided a descrip-

*W.E.B. Du Bois, *Black Folk Then and Now,* google.com/books /edition/Black_Folk_Then_and_Now_The_Oxford_W_E_B/kXTi AgAAQBAJ.

tion of this in his 1860 book, *A Pilgrimage to My Motherland*. During his time there he held a meeting with a ruler named Kumi. When Campbell arrived for the meeting, Kumi was not there. Campbell gave the following description of how the drummers used their drums to summon Kumi to the palace: "He was not at home when we reached his palace, but his officials received us kindly, and promised to call him immediately, which one of them did by making a loud peculiar noise with a drum, which, with its drummer, is kept for this and similar purposes. These drummers can, we learned, communicate, nay, converse with each other at any distance within the sound of the instrument."* Kumi arrived a few minutes later, having heard the noise from the drum.

There were medical advancements in Africa as well. One particular example of this was in the 1700s, when a physician named Cotton Mather was able to save lives during a smallpox outbreak in Boston. Mather utilized a technique for smallpox inoculation that he learned from his slave Onesimus. Onesimus was born in Africa and had been inoculated against smallpox while he was in Africa. Three hundred people in Africa had been inoculated using the same method. This inoculation technique significantly reduced the death rate from smallpox.

Timbuktu in West Africa is the site of one of the oldest centers of learning in the world. The University of Timbuktu pro-

---

*Robert Campbell, *A Pilgrimage to My Motherland*, google .com/books/edition/A_Pilgrimage_to_My_Motherland/3iRO AAAAcAAJ.

duced hundreds of thousands of manuscripts dating back to the fourteenth century. These writings covered a variety of topics such as history, mathematics, astronomy, medicine, and geography. One of the best-known scholars from the University of Timbuktu was Ahmed Baba. He was the author of more than forty books.

In the precolonial period Africans managed to build large monuments, engaged in metallurgy, developed methods of long-distance communication, developed medical advancements such as smallpox inoculation, and developed universities. The colonial period was a period of stagnation for Africa. This was because the colonial administrations were not concerned with Africa's development. The colonial powers of Europe utilized Africa's resources for the benefit of Europe, while doing little to develop Africa.

Vibranium does not exist in the real world, but Africa does produce resources that contributed greatly to the development of Western societies. Firestone Rubber Company, for example, built a fortune from Liberia's rubber. Copper mined from Africa was used to produce electrical equipment such as wires, motors, and power lines. The first atomic bomb was produced using uranium mined from the Belgian Congo. All of these are just some examples of how Africa's vast resources were used to advance Western societies during the colonial period.

By escaping colonialism, Wakanda was free to utilize its resources to develop the nation in ways that were beneficial to the Wakandans. The advanced technology of Wakanda is the very thing used to hide the country. Wakanda is hidden behind a large hologram that projects a massive forest to outsiders. The technology of Wakanda also led to medical advancements. When Everett Ross is shot in the back, he is taken to Wakanda, where Shuri treats him by utilizing medical technology that can completely heal a bullet wound. The Black Panther suit itself is another example of Wakanda's advanced technology. In the film, Shuri provides some updates to the suit. One of the updates allows the suit to absorb kinetic energy. To make the suit easy to transport, Shuri designed the suit to be able to fit inside T'Challa's necklace. This is all made possible by the fact that Wakandans have complete control over their vibranium supply.

Despite all these technological advancements, Wakanda is still rooted in its traditional culture. The people of Wakanda practice their own traditional religion, which centers around the worship of a panther god and the veneration of ancestors. Wakanda's government is overseen by a monarch who governs with a council of advisors, which includes tribal leaders and the queen mother, Ramonda. Wakanda challenges the notion that modernization in Africa requires rejecting traditional African culture in favor of Western cultural traditions by presenting a technologically advanced nation that also retains its own traditional culture. The Wakandans do not need to be "civilized" through the influence of a foreign European culture in order to build a technologically advanced society.

Wakanda's depiction in *Black Panther* challenges the way that Africa has been traditionally portrayed in popular movies throughout the years. These movies have often dehumanized Africans by portraying them as obstacles to be overcome by foreign protagonists. For example, *Trader Horn* is a 1931 film about two white travelers who rescue a white woman who was kidnapped by an African tribe. *The Naked Prey* (1965) is about a white man who is hunted down like prey by an African tribe that is trying to kill him. *King Solomon's Mines* (1985) includes a scene in which the two white protagonists are captured by a cannibal African tribe, which tries to cook them in a large pot. Africans in these films are depicted as unruly savages and the protagonists in these films must struggle for their survival against these vicious African tribes.

Even films that are based on historical events in Africa tend to portray Africans in a dehumanizing manner. *Zulu* is a 1964 film that depicted the historic Battle of Rorke's Drift between the British and the Zulus. The film focused on the British perspective of the conflict and presented the British as heroically overcoming the Zulus. The Zulus in this movie are simply fierce foes for the British soldiers to overcome. *Zulu* depicted the British conquest of the Zulus, but not the consequences of that conquest. The audience is not shown the death and destruction that the British conquest of the Zulus caused. Instead, *Zulu* ends with a scene in which the defeated Zulus sing a song to honor the bravery of the British soldiers. *Zulu* was released at a time when apartheid was still in place in South Africa. European colonizers had not only conquered Africans in South Africa but also maintained control over the land and resources there through racist policies that restricted the rights of Africans. Yet *Zulu* still portrayed the British soldiers in the war as brave fighters who earned the respect of the very people that they conquered.

The 2001 film *Black Hawk Down* was based on the real-life Battle of Mogadishu between American and Somali combatants. Much like *Zulu*, *Black Hawk Down* is presented from the perspective of the foreign soldiers, rather than the native Africans. As such, the American soldiers are depicted more sympathetically than the Somali fighters are. Whenever an American soldier is killed in combat, the film focuses on the impact of the moment. For example, the dying words of one American soldier are, "Tell my girls I'll be okay." There is another scene where the American soldiers desperately try to save a wounded soldier who eventually succumbs to his injury. Somalis, on the other hand, are simply presented as enemies for the American soldiers. There is little sympathy shown for the scores of Somalis who are killed in the battle. The audience does not see the Somali soldiers express concern for their families or mourn the loss of their comrades. *Black Hawk Down* never explores the suffering and the loss of the Somalis in the same way that the suffering and loss of the Americans are portrayed.

The suffering and death caused by colonialism were mostly treated with indifference by the colonial powers because colonizers did not view Africans as being real people. They instead viewed Africans as objects who either stood in the way of the goals of the colonizers or as objects who could be ruthlessly exploited to advance the goals of the colonizers. The dehumanizing portrayal of Africans in these films reflects the dehumanizing way that colonizers viewed African people.

Black Panther not only portrays a technologically advanced African society but also, and perhaps more important, portrays Africans as humans. Wakandans are presented as real people with motives and personal struggles. T'Challa is the newly crowned king of Wakanda who is still struggling with the loss of his father. T'Challa is also torn between upholding Wakanda's centuries-old tradition of isolationism and using its technology for the benefit of others. This conflict is established early in the movie when T'Challa tracks down his former girlfriend, Nakia. He finds Nakia in Nigeria rescuing a group of women who have been captured. Nakia believes that Wakanda should be doing more to assist others, but T'Challa is reluctant because he insists on upholding Wakanda's tradition. Tradition is very important to T'Challa, but when he is forced to confront the unintended consequences of Wakanda's isolationism, he finally rejects this policy.

Killmonger is an antagonist who is driven by a desire for revenge for what the previous Black Panther did to Killmonger and his father. Killmonger's desire for vengeance is so strong that he kills without mercy. He is even willing to sacrifice those who are close to him to achieve his goal, but Killmonger is not presented as an unsympathetic killer. *Black Panther* explores why Killmonger became the way that he is. Killmonger is hardened by his experiences, but he is not emotionless, as we see in the scene when Killmonger sheds tears after he reunites with his father on the ancestral plane.

What makes Killmonger an especially complex villain is that he is motivated by a desire to save others. Whereas T'Challa is content to keep Wakanda hidden away from the rest of the world, Killmonger desires to utilize Wakanda's technology to assist African people who have not been fortunate enough to have escaped the hardships of colonialism and racism like the Wakandans have been able to do. T'Challa objects to Killmonger's violent methods, but T'Challa ultimately accepts that utilizing Wakanda's technology for the benefit of others is the correct thing to do.

It is noteworthy that characters such as N'Jobu, Nakia, and Killmonger are compelled to question Wakanda's policy of isolation because of their experiences outside of Wakanda. Wakanda is so isolated that those who live there seem removed from the struggles of African people in the rest of the world. In his dying remarks, when Killmonger refers to his ancestors who jumped into the ocean because they viewed death as being better than slavery, he is referring to his ancestors from his mother's side, because the people of Wakanda were never stolen from their homeland and enslaved in a strange land, nor did they have to endure the experience of being colonized and exploited in their own land. Wakandans are unburdened by these struggles. This helps the audience to envision a society where African people do not have to be burdened by the challenges that stem from the legacy of slavery and colonialism.

In *Black Panther,* Wakanda is presented as a nation that has the capacity to change the world. This is one of the central plot points of the film, but *Black Panther*'s presentation of Wakanda provides more than just a narrative that drives the conflict between T'Challa and Killmonger. Wakanda provides a vision for what could be for Africa. Of course, Wakanda is a fictional representation. In the real world there is no Wakanda. There is no African nation that has remained untouched by European conquests and colonial domination, but this does not mean that a technologically advanced African state is not possible. Africa certainly has the resources for this, and Africa's history demonstrates that Africans do have the capacity to develop advanced civilizations. In this regard, Wakanda not only challenges Western stereotypes about Africa but also provides a depiction of Africa's potential.

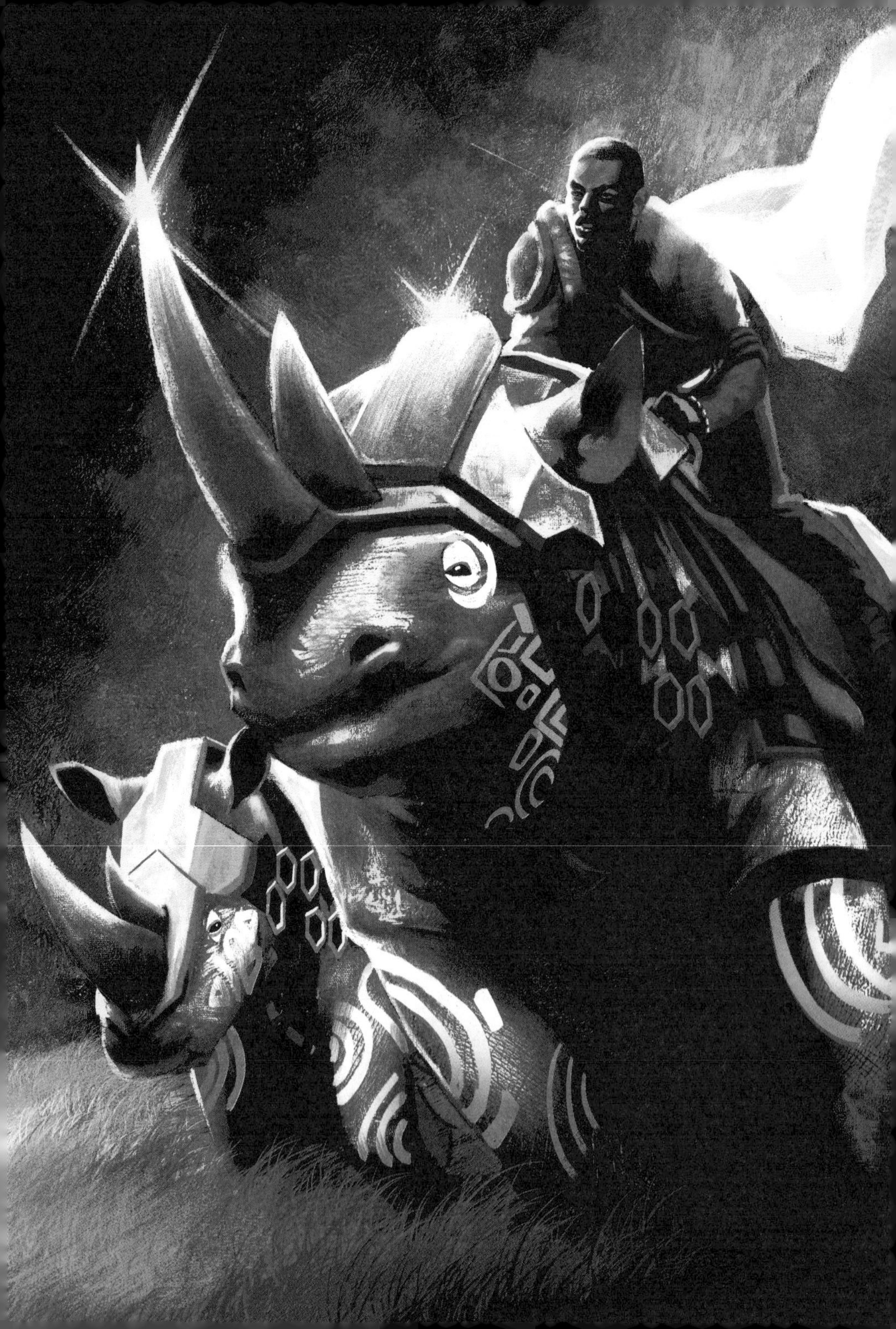

WAKANDA: A DOOR AJAR

Suyi Davies Okungbowa, author, professor, and
contributor to *Black Panther: Tales of Wakanda*

I N EVERY COLLEGE class I teach, I like to introduce my students to authors and stories from beyond their typical purview. This often includes at least one piece of speculative fiction from an author of African descent, especially those that imagine alternative existences and center Blackness in their vision. Often, many of these teens—majority white, of some privilege, and with limited knowledge of the world beyond their immediate social groups—are excited by the fact that they get to experience stories centering peoples and places they've only ever heard about in passing, particularly of or inspired by the African continent and its diasporas. Many have been pre-loaded with the singular story of Africa as a poor, "dark" continent with minimal to no history, and a decent number are interested in hearing something new.

During such a class—*every* such class—someone inevitably mentions *Black Panther.*

Not the popular Marvel comic that has run for decades, no.

The 2018 film written by Ryan Coogler and Joe Robert Cole. Prior to becoming a professor of creative writing in North America, I did not know much about the history of the comic and the character myself. Not until I read up right before the movie came out (and then contributed to *Tales of Wakanda,* the first-ever collection of short stories based on the character).

Much of this can be attributed to limited access to U.S.-produced comics when I was a young man growing up in Nigeria, even though I sought heroes who looked like me. A combination of various factors, including the historical marginalization of work centering authors of African descent, meant that many of us for whom the existence of the Black Panther was a shining light in a dark mediascape didn't even get to hear much about him before 2018.

But then came the Marvel movie, and suddenly none of that mattered anymore. *Black Panther* started as a movie, but quickly became a moment. People of African descent, no matter where they were situated on the globe, were enthralled and supportive. From elderly parents to young kids, people who had never once seen themselves heralded and celebrated as super heroes on the big screen suddenly had found a new Black hero to identify with. And not just us—even various non-Black people who had tired of seeing the same super heroes on TV were glad to witness a breath of fresh air.

It is this power I think about whenever my students bring up *Black Panther:* that one story possesses the ability to generate a shared sense of camaraderie for a varied set of people, many of whom may have never come in contact with one another. The existence of *Black Panther* opens up more room for conversation within global speculative fiction, but also for critical discourse. Within the sliver of light shining through this little door nudged ajar lies opportunities for convergence and understanding, a possibility for engagement, deeper thinking, and critical analysis of the state of global Blackness. A movie turned moment turned movement.

STEPPING THROUGH THE CRACK

In classes when I'm specifically teaching about Afrocentric futurisms, I often take the time to show the full *Black Panther* movie. It is an opportunity to demonstrate to my students that there is room for critical engagement and discourse (not to mention lessons in good storytelling) even within material we already enjoy and consume for leisure. As we watch the film, we pause it periodically and discuss the various opportunities for us to engage with the history and contemporary state of global Blackness and Afro-ness. We attempt to grapple alongside Killmonger, analyzing his choices to determine if we would make better ones. We interrogate N'Jobu's and T'Challa's and W'Kabi's decisions, searching for useful reasoning behind why they would think as they do. We dissect the undercarriage of T'Chaka's aphorisms and raise questions about what histories these proverbs and statements tap into. We discuss the roles of Okoye and Nakia and the Dora Milaje, and the successes (or failures) of feminist ideas and ideals outside of dominant Western positioning. We draw parallels between the employment of resources like the Heart-Shaped Herb and vibranium and the struggles we encounter with our society's use of comparable resources—for good causes and otherwise.

What this does is teach students not only how to ask questions, but also how to engage with difficult material that they are not always familiar with and do not always agree with. *Black Panther* becomes more than just a movie or moment: It becomes a pathway to reminding us that the classroom is a community of learning, and it is possible to enjoy ourselves as we learn. A door once shut is now nudged ajar, and through it we may begin to access more material that, on a typical day, would not receive as much interest.

One of the often-overlooked impacts of the *Black Panther* movie is the space it creates for fiction from and about the African continent and its diasporas to be read less like anthropological study texts. Here is a story about a super hero and the kingdom he protects, powered by magic and science—no different from Captain America or Spider-Man. And while these stories contain social commentary, they are first and foremost fun stories for people to enjoy and discuss on the playground or at the water cooler, reasons to collect figurines and buy merch.

This kind of freedom has not often been offered to stories centering people of African descent, which are often presented as texts to learn about the people and/or culture first, and less about the fun, super hero ways of being. When stories of people of African descent are discussed, it is often a deep-seated excavation of matters of poverty, crime, migration, violence, corruption, evil religious practices, and more. But *Black Panther* offers entertainment and fun. Though there are discussions of matters like imperialism and colonialism, the movie still provides us with

Shuri's cool Panther suit designs, war rhinos, the Dora Milaje's exciting spears, Nakia's exceptional combat skills. All the *fictional* and *fun* and *cool* stuff that's simply made to be enjoyed, just like any other piece of media from anywhere else in the world.

A DIVERSITY OF VOICES

The *Black Panther* viewing in my classes serves to reinforce the fact I've raised above: that stories centering Africans and Afrodescendant peoples can be *multiple* things at once. Which is why, right after the viewing, I slip through this crack now opened, taking the opportunity to point my students toward other work from authors and scholars of African descent, saying: *Oh, look, there's more where that came from.* Many expect that I will simply bring forth other stories like *Black Panther,* but I instead offer works that range in form and approach.

We discuss scholars like Samuel R. Delany; read Mark Dery's interviews with him, Greg Tate, and Tricia Rose; and talk about the birth of the term "Afrofuturism" in North America. We talk about how that term has warped and changed, and we discuss sibling expressions like Reynaldo Anderson's "Afrofuturism 2.0 & 3.0," Nnedi Okorafor's "Africanfuturism," Minister Faust's "Africentrism," Martine Syms's "Mundane Afrofuturist Manifesto." We read and discuss stories and essays from authors and scholars like Octavia Butler, Nalo Hopkinson, Kojo Laing, N. K. Jemisin, T. L. Huchu, Dilman Dila, Sheree Renée Thomas, Nnedi Okorafor, Ytasha Womack, Kodwo Eshun, Nisi Shawl, Tananarive Due, Ibi Zoboi, Karen Lord, Tochi Onyebuchi, Lesley Nneka Arimah, Wanuri Kahiu, P. Djèlí Clark, Eugen Bacon, Tade Thompson, etc. We engage with art and artists across media that incorporate the consciousness of Afrocentric futurisms and other alternate realities in their work like Janelle Monáe, Beyoncé, Missy Elliott, Ibeyi, Jojo Abot, Ibaaku, Petite Noir, Lil' Nas X, and Osborne Macharia. We read author roundtables, like that featured in Isiah Lavender III and Lisa Yaszek's *Literary Afrofuturism in the Twenty-First Century*. We analyze critical scholarly debates, disagreements, and complications like those presented in *African Literature Today 39: Speculative and Science Fiction*. More often than not, at the end of the course students come away with more than a cursory understanding of the various imaginations possible that center Africans and Afrodescendants.

This understanding is important because there also exist disagreements as to the effect of the *Black Panther* movie. Whether there is truth to these oppositions or not is moot, as such complication is the point of the film. As *The New Yorker* staff writer Jelani Cobb puts it in his review: "The implicit statement in both the film's themes and its casting is that there is a connection, however vexed, tenuous, and complicated, among the continent's scattered descendants." This is similar to the position I have often offered when asked: that the very presence of complication in the identification of the African and/or Afrodescendant self, no matter how far removed from the continent by distance and/or time, is a blessing. Deconstructing the singular story of the dark continent requires such complication, which produces mess. And mess, indeed, is a part of making. If the fictional Wakanda serves as a door ajar, offering space for more voices, stories, theories, and disagreements to slip through and be heard, I say we are better for it. A diversity of voices, after all, is the antidote to the single story.

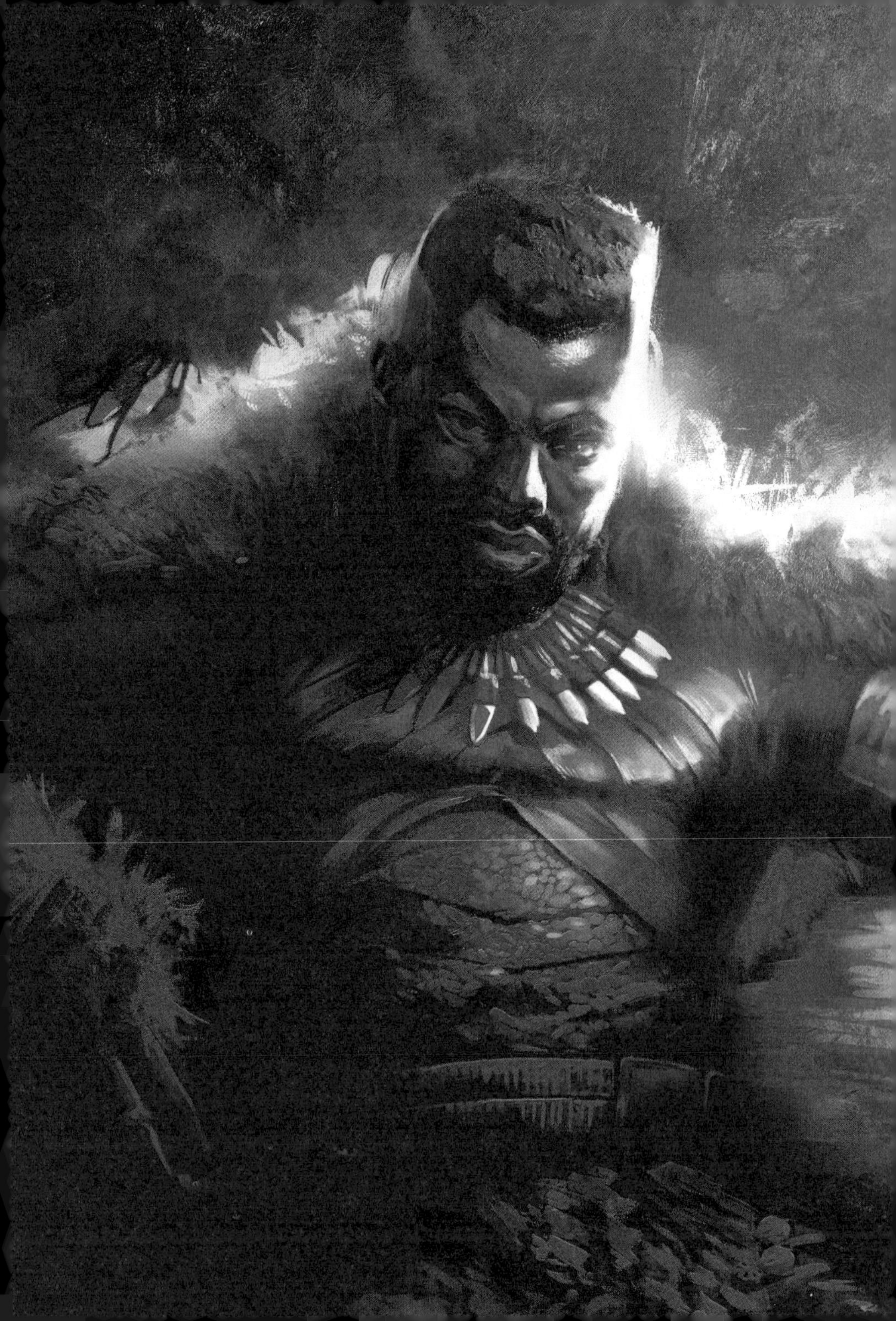

THE POWER OF IMAGINATION: *BLACK PANTHER'S* IMPACT ON BLACK YOUTH

◇◇

Arvell Jones, teacher, entrepreneur,
graphic designer, and comics creator

I HAVE BEEN A fan of Marvel Comics' Black Panther since his creation. I was a nerd before nerds were called nerds. One day in the seventh grade, I carried a comic book to school, and back then that was certain to get you targeted for lunch money confiscation and harassment. When I was approached for my near-daily contribution to the "feed-a-thug fund," a member of the group asked, "Why do you read these silly comic books?" I then explained to them who the Black man was on the cover of that introductory issue of *Fantastic Four #52*. They kept the book, but to my surprise, they let me go. Black Panther saved me from getting beaten up that day. Two weeks later they were buying comics themselves and giving my comic books back to me.

Black Panther motivated me to create my own super heroes of color. Living in a world of fantasy and fiction, I would allow my imagination to get the best of me. At first, that meant pretending that I was one of my make-believe characters, someone whom I could emulate. I would daydream during classes about what he or she would look like and what type of costumes they would wear; then I would create other characters. I spent so much time sketching and creating stories, including some for *Black Panther,* but with my own characters. I was so inspired; I knew I had to be in an environment to help me further my dreams. I wanted to be around like-minded people and learn from the best, so I got involved with comic fandom. I began going to early comic book conventions, which led me to work on the Detroit Triple Fan Fair, one of the first large comic cons in the nation.

In April 1973, I went to work for Marvel Comics in New York City, when Stan Lee was still working there, at 625 Madison Avenue. I worked as an art assistant to Richard (Rich) Buckler, who was the artist on *Jungle Action* #6, the very issue that featured Black Panther and introduced Erik Killmonger, written by Don McGregor. When the *Black Panther* movie was announced many years later, I was more than a little excited for several reasons. I was finally going to see a strong Black man, an African who looked like me with a rich heritage I could be proud of. He was responsible for his kingdom, one of the most technologically advanced countries in the world. A powerful hero who was not only physically strong, but brave, optimistic, and hopeful. He stood for justice and was someone the Black community could look up to. Unlike any other Marvel Studios film debut, *Black Panther* attracted a huge buzz among many communities, including those in the city I returned to, Detroit, Michigan.

Before I could make plans to go to the debut showing of the film, I was contacted by a couple of local organizations that were holding screenings in and around Detroit. The one that attracted me the most was Alkebu-lan Village, a local community center that my daughter had previously attended for several years. Alkebu-lan (which took its name from an ancient term for Africa) was initially a martial arts organization that evolved into a culture-based institution founded on African principles. Over 200,000 youth and families have walked through the doors of Alkebu-lan Village for after-school programs, African-centered education, martial arts studies, computer classes, professional development, African dance, multimedia, photography, videography, and many more educational programs and community-building initiatives.

Black Panther was in line with Alkebu-lan Village's African-centered philosophy to "live in harmony with yourself and others by learning and teaching self-respect, self-discipline, self-control and self-defense." Alkebu-lan rented the only independent movie house in the city of Detroit and hosted the local premiere of *Black Panther*.

What seemed like just another entry in a parade of super hero movies was much more. It was wonderful. The local affair that was held in Detroit reestablished a cultural footprint that is enormous to the African American community. African American youth growing up in the inner city got a chance to see the Kingdom of Wakanda reenacted within the City of Detroit. From the attire to the conversations, the culture was inspired and influenced. I saw young girls dressed as *Black Panther*'s royal guards, the Dora Milaje. They were standing in formation as moviegoers entered the lobby of the theater. Local dignitaries from Wayne County, the City of Detroit, and the Detroit Public Schools Community District participated in and attended the event. There was even an awards ceremony that recognized local talent. For me, it all highlighted the vision of the movie. This experience had a positive impact on the lives of the kids for years to come. The film gave them a mission, and Alkebu-lan Village offered them a chance to exercise this new sense of pride, community, and self-esteem.

Experiencing the impact of *Black Panther* on inner-city youth was a full-circle moment for me. Sitting in the audience, I surveyed the theater and saw pure joy and excitement as the kids were fully engaged in the movie, watching T'Challa, Shuri, Nakia, and the Dora Milaje overcome the challenges presented in the film. It reminded me of those thugs, now friends, back in the day—of seeing their excitement about reading the comic books, just like the kids in the theater. After the screening I was amused to see parents gathered to react to the film, as if no one wanted to leave. I watched as those who ran the community center germinated the seeds to adapt several of the concepts from the film, using it as a tool to instill the guiding principles of African culture.

The instructors at Alkebu-lan Village are licensed professionals, and the organization's African philosophy is reflected in the seven principles of Kwanzaa, or Nguzo Saba:

1. *UMOJA,* UNITY: To strive for and maintain unity in the family, community, nation, and race.
2. *KUJICHAGULIA,* SELF-DETERMINATION: To define ourselves, name ourselves, create for ourselves, and speak for ourselves.

3. *UJIMA*, COLLECTIVE WORK AND RESPONSIBILITY: To build and maintain our community, make our brothers' and sisters' problems our problems, and solve them together.

4. *UJAMAA*, COOPERATIVE ECONOMICS: To build and maintain our own stores, shops, and other businesses and to profit from them together.

5. *NIA*, PURPOSE: To make our collective vocation the building and developing of our community in order to restore our people to their traditional greatness.

6. *KUUMBA*, CREATIVITY: To always do as much as we can, in the way we can, in order to leave our community more beautiful and beneficial than we inherited it.

7. *IMANI*, FAITH: To believe with all our hearts in our people, our parents, our teachers, our leaders, and the righteousness and victory of our struggle.

These core principles, linked to the film in numerous ways, are memorized and recited daily at Alkebu-lan Village.

Marvis Cofield, executive director and CEO, and Larry Green, president of Alkebu-lan Martial Arts Association, used *Black Panther* as inspiration to empower the community. After the premiere, people of all ages participated in workshops about the movie. They learned how *Black Panther* came about, why it is important to have Black heroes, and that as Black people, we can draw inspiration from these stories, whether they are real or imagined. The children wanted to learn more about Africa and its history, to understand what their African names mean, to take Swahili classes, and to visit the Charles H. Wright African American Museum in Detroit to learn about their ancestry. Overall, the film provided an opportunity for children to see people who looked like them working together to honor and protect their community.

In popular media, those of us who are not white have more trouble finding representation of ourselves. There were not nearly enough role models and super heroes when I was a kid— the Black characters on television and in movies were primarily portrayed as buffoons or clowns, which made me feel ashamed of my dark skin. Aside from Sidney Poitier and Harry Belafonte, who were represented with strength, dignity, and pride, I did not see many Black role models in the media, and especially not super heroes.

When my children were growing up in the 2000s, they had some role models that they looked up to, but there were still no super heroes they could imagine themselves as. Now that they are adults, *Black Panther* showed them that it is possible for Black men and women to lead a blockbuster super hero film.

As a nerdy seventh grader, I couldn't have imagined how much Black Panther would impact my own life, let alone the lives of millions of children around the world. I'm sure the future of Black Panther will continue to address the need for more inclusion and inspire young girls and boys, as well as adults, to see themselves as powerful. The movie *Black Panther* sparked and expanded the imaginations of many children while teaching valuable lessons and setting up principles to live by. After all, it's the imagination that sparks innovation, and that is the very thing that improves the world.

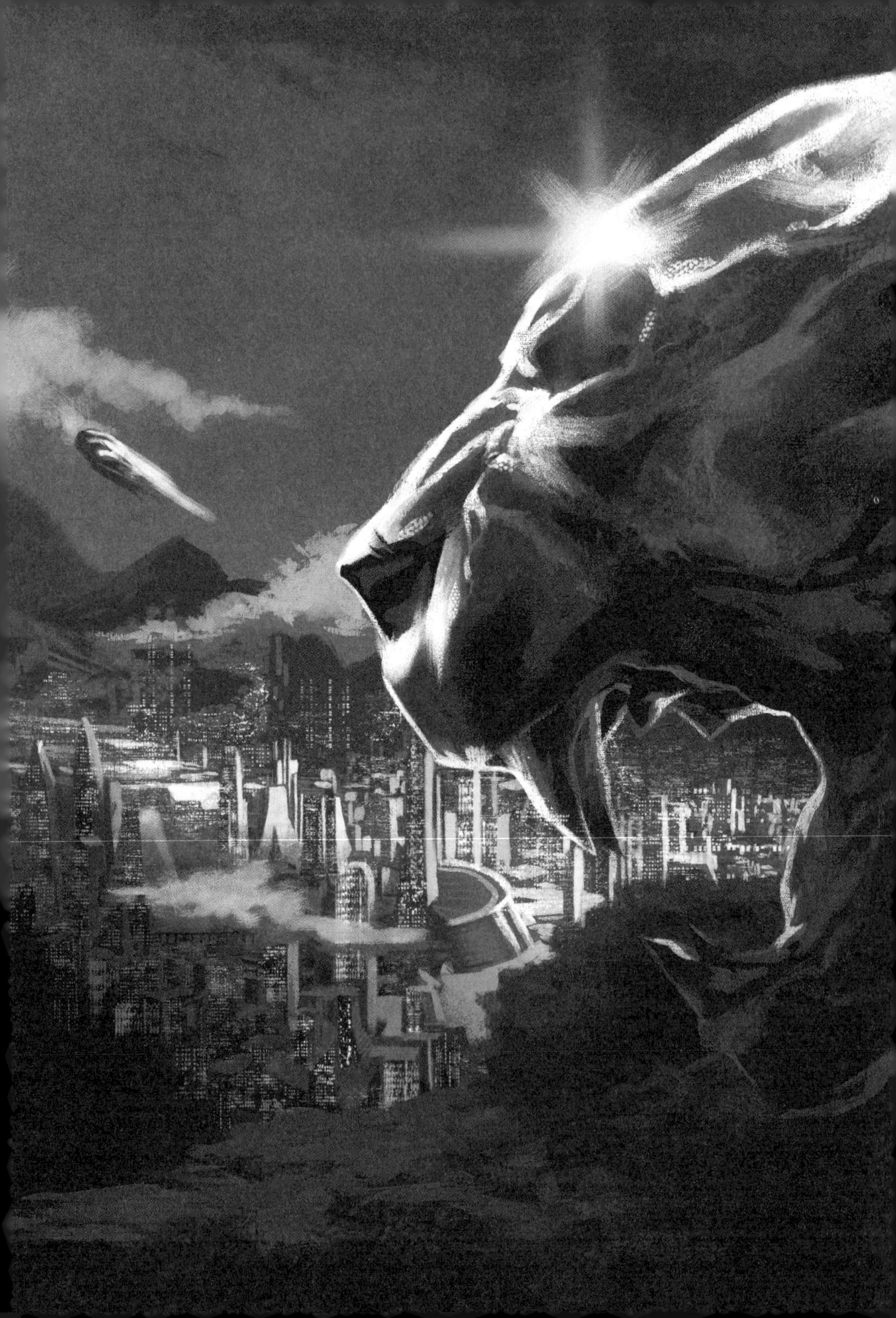

DARING TO DREAM OF
A BLACK UTOPIA

◇

Maurice Broaddus, writer, community organizer, teacher,
and contributor to Marvel Comics'
Black Panther: Tales of Wakanda

When we say Wakanda it means [forget] your dress codes
It means do not tell us to be quiet
It means we know racism as well as the moon knows
    its first crater
And we do not fear making waves
          —COREY EWING, "WHEN WE SAY WAKANDA"

A HUNDRED YEARS AGO, Colonel Allen Allensworth had a dream. A former slave and later an Army chaplain, he had a vision for what a flat, barren stretch of California could be: a utopian colony of, by, and for African Americans. A sanctuary for those he called "the masses who are without opportunity and without hope," a place that could serve as an escape from the reach of Jim Crow and lynchings. And people responded, with many of the "Black Okies"—the 40,000 Black migrants who moved to California in the 1930s and '40s to build a better life in the West—flocking there. And for many years, the dream, the shared vision, was a reality.

That's the thing about dreams. They help us imagine different ways of being and moving in this world. Many of the problems we face as a society seem insurmountable largely because there is a collective failure of imagination. Often artists and their creations have to pave the way by presenting possibilities. As the reaction to the movie *Black Panther* and its depiction of Wakanda shows, the idea of a utopia—a longing for something better—continues to live in the human imagination.

What is a utopia?

With the rise and predominance of Western political theory, the idea of utopia has been wrestled with almost from its inception. In his work *The Republic* (ca. 375 B.C.E.), Plato considers the meaning of justice, examines the types of regimes at the time, and proposes different hypothetical ways of rule, including the importance of philosophy and poetry in society. Sir Thomas More's *Utopia* (1516) depicts a fictional island society and its religious, social, and political customs. Though an incomplete novel, Francis Bacon's *New Atlantis* (1627) portrays a land centered on "generosity and enlightenment, dignity and splendor, piety and public spirit" as the central quality of its inhabitants. The concepts and ideals are aspirational. Even the notion of "the American Dream" is a stab at the utopian ideal of a (representative) democracy that centers inalienable rights, liberty, opportunity, and equality. Yet it is a dream waiting to come to fruition.

But we must go from among our oppressors; [liberation] never can be done by staying among them.

—Martin R. Delany

The idea of a Black utopia has danced in the imaginations of African Americans from the beginning. It is an ideal rooted in Black imagination. From the time of the Maafa, the holocaust known as chattel slavery, as Africans were brought to Western shores in chains, there has been the desire, drive, and dream of a better life. Such dreaming is what we've always done to survive and cope with intergenerational trauma, the weight of history, betrayal by the law, and the inequities of economic systems. We've clung to the hope of seeking emancipation from predatory systems and ways of being in order to pursue a collective life based in identity and shared story. We have yearned to create a space defined by self-determination, self-sufficiency, self-government, and self-improvement. History is filled with such experiments, such as the maroon communities, where descendants of Africans in the Americas formed settlements away from slavery; small enclaves of intentional communities such as M.O.V.E. (Philadelphia, Pennsylvania); or independent Black communities like Mound Bayou (Mississippi), Lyles Station (Indiana), Seneca Village (New York), and Tulsa (Oklahoma), home to "Black Wall Street."

On the periphery of our cultural imagination lies Wakanda.

First appearing in Marvel's comic book *Fantastic Four* #52, Wakanda was created by Stan Lee and Jack Kirby in 1966 (unrelatedly, the Black Panther Party also launched that year). Somewhere in East Africa, it is the most technologically advanced country on the planet, with the foremost military, thanks to its possession and use of the element vibranium. It is a country shrouded in mystery and mysticism; isolated, though technologically advanced. Its people have a high degree of civic pride, with a culture that defines and reinforces their identity. In Wakanda, organized around resources and free from the history of oppression, there is peace and prosperity.

THE RISE OF AFROFUTURISM

Speculative art has long been entwined with African American concerns and themes, telling stories about culture, technology, and how things could be. In 1993, in his essay "Black to the Future," Mark Dery coined the term "Afrofuturism" as a lament that more African Americans weren't active in the field of sci-fi. He noted that, to his knowledge, only authors Samuel R. Delany, Octavia E. Butler, Steven Barnes, and Charles Saunders worked within the genre. Afrofuturism critiques the present by being rooted in the past and looking to the future. But the imagining of Black-centered worlds has been going on for much longer.

Martin R. Delany wrote *Blake; or the Huts of America* (1859), the story of a global slave insurrection that was Pan-African in scope, following Black migration to Central America, South America, and Africa. George Schuyler's *Black Empire* (1938) details an attempt by Black radicals to establish their own independent nation in Africa.

In music, Sun Ra (born Herman Blount on his way to Le Sony'r Ra) was an avant-garde jazz composer who reimagined himself. He saw the infinite potentialities of the Black experience and believed that we ought to seek new worlds for ourselves among the stars. With a nod to an Egyptian past that predated the Western world of the Greeks—his fashion being a spacesuit by way of Pharaoh's closet—he named his band the Arkestra and sonically traveled the universe. Even in practice, he created a culture of discipline, using communal living to forge a community and instill an ethos of helping others imagine something different for themselves.

Parliament-Funkadelic's funk wasn't just a type of music, it was a state of being. The band was the "home of the extraterrestrial brothers," as the introduction to their seminal 1975 album, *Mothership Connection,* says. They envisioned a space age that centers Black people, spun tales of Chocolate City, and portrayed a world where Black people were the cultural arbiters charting our own future. Their looks and sounds fused Black culture, iconography, and the future.

Octavia E. Butler's 1993 prophetic work, *Parable of the Sower,* describes a world beset by climate collapse, wealth inequity, and political demagoguery. Behind the dystopian world the book describes is the utopia that resides in its shadow: a community of hope and resilience.

In this context, the idea of Wakanda casts its own significant shadow.

After his debut in *Fantastic Four,* Black Panther's next appearance was in the early 1970s comic *Jungle Action,* written by Don McGregor and illustrated by Black artist Billy Graham. During its short run, such characters as Killmonger were created. However, in the 1990s, the importance and opportunity of having a Black voice define the Black Panther and chart the course of Wakanda came together.

For the master's tools will never dismantle the master's house. They may allow us temporarily to beat him at his own game, but they will never enable us to bring about genuine change.

—AUDRE LORDE

Christopher J. Priest, the first Black full-time writer to work at Marvel, reinvented *Black Panther* with his canonical run. Expounding on the technology, culture, and history, he was the first writer to approach Black Panther not as a super hero but as a king, bringing together tribal politics, the Dora Milaje, swagger, coolness, cultural commentary, and humor. Then came Reginald Hudlin (and Black Panther's marriage to Storm), Roxane Gay, Ta-Nehisi Coates (exploring the painful reality of how countries are forged), and John Ridley.

The Afrofuturist lens is visioning rooted in Black history and culture. It's a statement about a mindset of creating desired future states in the present. It reimagines how community moves through the world. The idea of Wakanda boils down to Black liberation on Black terms, representing a place fairly untouched by colonial influence. Ryan Coogler based aspects of his film version on Lesotho for that reason. Wakanda's magnificent, towering buildings, advanced technology, wealth, and vibranium do not make it a utopia. Access to resources does not make a society healthy, wealthy, or happy. What sets Wakanda apart is how its society functions.

Wakanda's leadership has a moral obligation to put its people's needs first. Prioritizing the hierarchy of needs—housing, food, health—allows its citizens the baseline to live full lives. Being in harmony with one another and nature (all of Wakanda's tech and progress being environmentally friendly) establishes a new rhythm of life.

And they enjoy peace.

Wakanda represents a place where culture fuels the imagination and drives practice, from history to ideas to philosophy to ways of being. Take fashion, for example. The film's bright palette and mixed-print ensembles are giving Black audiences new ways to cosplay. Clothing represents another form of storytelling, where the individual tells the world who they are. In Wakanda, it is not just self-expression but the sartorial imagination of a community's expression, be it the royal family, the Dora Milaje, scientists, or the various tribes. Their dress tells of how they honor their ancestors. Tells that they know who they are and their place in the world. Tells that they are proudly Wakandan.

Wakanda's cultural norms and etiquette embody a human-centered ecosystem, one that heals the sickness of the oppressive systems that plague most societies. It is a place where art is valued as much as science—though both are esteemed—because their aesthetics are political; their visions are political. Just by simply . . . being. Radical political ideas such as education, healthcare for the poor, redistribution of wealth, justice, and equity are prioritized by a system and government that sees their people's full humanity and values that over everything else.

Afrofuturist imaginations speculate about how technology intersects with culture. After all, technology is also a cultural instrument used to build the future. Futuristic technology abounds in Wakanda—self-piloting aircraft and cars, remotely operated planes, maglev trains, holographic displays, kimoyo beads. Wakanda provides a visualization of critical engagement with science and technology. Shuri herself sends a strong signal to young girls, providing representation of them as scientists, inventors, or engineers. Such modeling is at the heart of Wakanda as a powerful image.

Yet they chose to isolate.

Isolation is a perfectly valid option for how Wakanda chose to initially interact with the world. Its very existence and the ideas on which it was built disrupt our thinking about how society should run. Add to that its wealth, advanced tech, and an unmatched military. All combine to make Wakanda an actual threat.

THE THREAT OF WAKANDA

Wakanda's mere existence represents a challenge to systems, from their caste structure to their practice of supremacy to how they distribute power. The dream, much less its embodied "reality," holds up a mirror. It announces that we don't have to keep doing things the way we've been doing them. That those who are in control don't have the final say in how we choose to be and live. That's a threat.

Wakanda's self-sufficiency and wealth imply that it doesn't have to participate in the world economy. It could very easily just be the kind of neighbor who erects fences and closes its garage door, letting everyone else fend for themselves. That would be selfish, rotting its own moral core by turning a blind eye to the suffering going on around it. But the fact that it can choose whether to interact, independent of anyone else, is a threat.

Wakanda is advanced and rich in resources, chief among them being vibranium. Its incredible technology also drives a huge portion of Wakanda's economy (for example, the time it bought out Stark Enterprises). Its advanced tech powers its military, giving it unrivaled defensive capability. All of this is driven by the country's control over most of the world's vibranium stores. The history of humanity is one of violence. Wars are fought over control of territory or resources. Having control of both makes Wakanda a threat.

Frankly, conquering the world would have been another valid option. But instead of choosing to perceive all of their neighbors as a potential threat, they chose the path of withdrawal. Being isolationist is safe, but there is an inherent harm to ignoring inequality and the plight of one's neighbor. Being a good neighbor, modeling what that means, only brings risk. But the Wakandans have come to the realization that they were never called to be safe. Wakanda isn't perfect: power is still concentrated in a royal family. People are still people, often ambitious, mistrusting, selfish, and fearful. There remains a tension between science and the sacred traditions. People differ on the best ways for the country to move forward, progressivism versus conservatism, in this complicated world. But that's also the power of the story: the ideal.

THE INSPIRING IDEA OF WAKANDA

There is a power to mythmaking, which America often employs with its Founding Fathers, American Dream, and Manifest Destiny. The story of Wakanda—what it represents to its citizens as well as us viewers/readers—speaks of the seemingly impossible. An overarching, aspirational story that creates a new framework of operating, that transforms, or at least recontextualizes, a Pan-African story.

The history of African Americans could rightly be described as dystopian. From the Maafa to Jim Crow to mass incarceration, a lot of our dreams have been conceived as reactions to our oppressors. The dream has to be rooted in a different way of being. The Black experience has been marked by the constant struggle to exist, to be considered fully human. Fighting for basic rights in pursuit of justice and equality. It's also why a world led by the marginalized is the surest path to building an inclusive world. No one knows better than the marginalized how unequal society has been and what it means to have to organize differently. To have a mindset trained in abundance, not scarcity. To have a clear sense of cultural nationalism and identity, respecting a shared story. To cultivate and center people's humanness and interconnectedness. And to leave room for emergence, having a respect for things not yet born.

In 2018, Aliaume Damala Badara Akon Thiam, the award-winning R&B singer best known as Akon, had a dream for a futuristic city. A real-life version of Wakanda built in his ancestral home, Senegal. A place that would incorporate the latest technologies and cryptocurrencies, embodying the future of an African society. Gifted 2,000 acres and raising over $6 billion, he laid the future Akon City's first stone.

Wakanda is a model to strive toward, a critique of how the affluent use their power. It still has to wrestle with its place in the world. We live in dark times—in a world broken by homophobia, xenophobia, racism, misogyny, patriarchy, war, and pandemics. Problems that require radical reimagining. The chaos of people's shattered reality allows opportunities for new pathways to help mend things. The idea of Wakanda, a Black-led utopia, gives us room to imagine, space to dream. Liberation lies at the intersection of art, politics, and agency, but it begins with our imagination. Wakanda fires our imaginations by charting possibilities enveloped in culture and ethos and practice. We begin to envision liberation, justice, equality, and a place where we are supported and pushed to be our best selves.

And that's how revolutions begin.

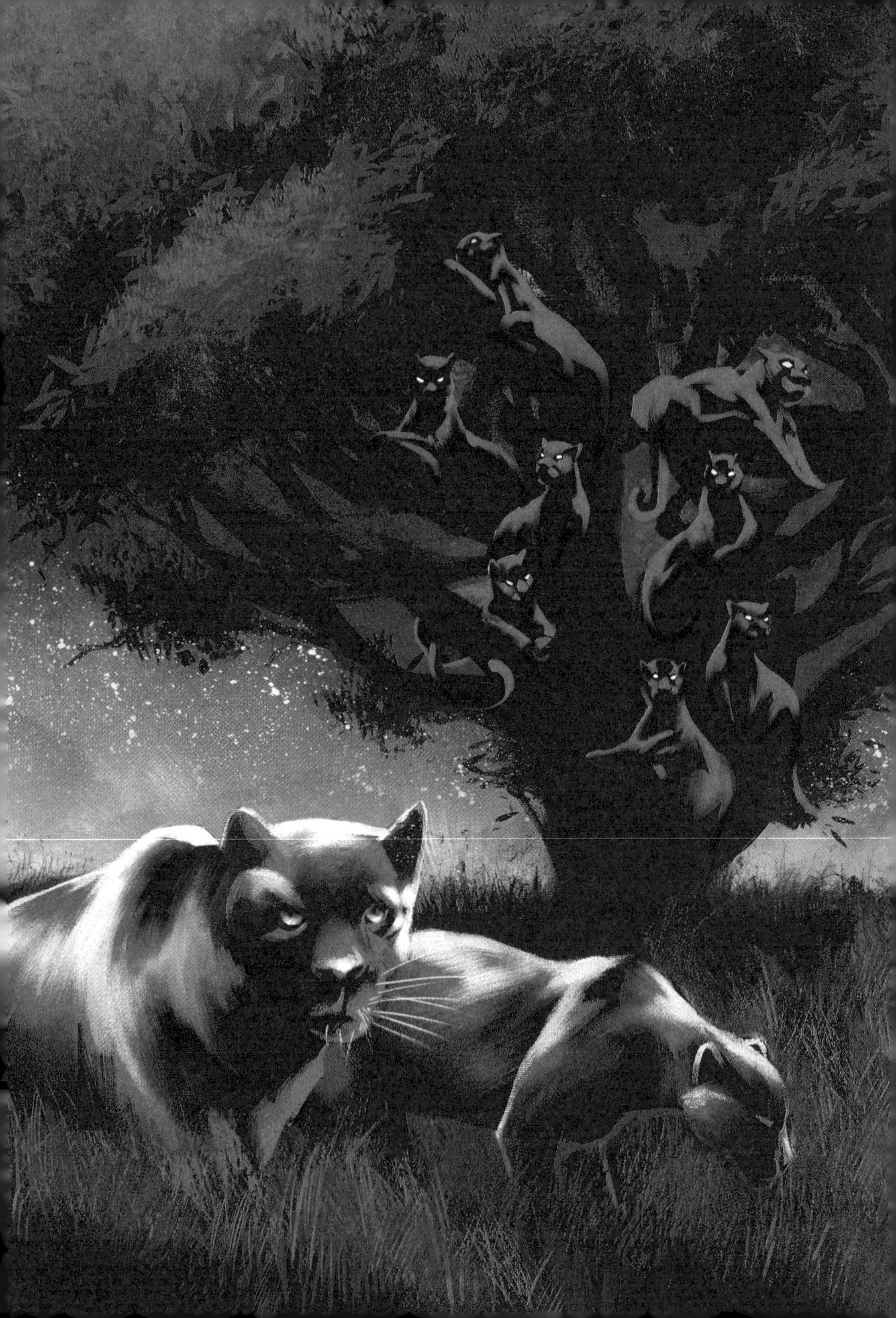

ABOUT THE CONTRIBUTORS

MARLENE ALLEN AHMED is an associate professor of English literature at United Arab Emirates University. She researches and writes about speculative fiction by African American authors such as Octavia Butler, Nalo Hopkinson, Tananarive Due, Justina Ireland, and Steven Barnes. She is also the co-editor of the book *Afterimages of Slavery: Essays on Appearances in Recent American Films, Literature, Television, and Other Media* (2012).

AARON C. ALLEN is an assistant professor of cultural studies at Roger Williams University in Bristol, RI. His research interests include critical race studies, critical university studies, and post-civil-rights racial politics. Dr. Allen is also a passionate teacher, providing students with a foundation to understand, speak about, and directly challenge structural inequities.

MAURICE BROADDUS is a community organizer and teacher. His work has appeared in places like *Lightspeed, Black Panther: Tales from Wakanda, Weird Tales, Magazine of F&SF,* and *Uncanny Magazine,* with some of his stories having been collected in *The Voices of Martyrs.* His books include the sci-fi novel *Sweep of Stars,* the steampunk works *Buffalo Soldier* and *Pimp My Airship,* and the middle-grade detective novels *The Usual Suspects* and *Unfadeable.* His project *Sorcerers* is being adapted as a television show for AMC. He's an editor at *Apex Magazine.* Learn more at MauriceBroaddus.com.

RUTH E. CARTER is the 2019 Academy Award winner in costume design for Marvel's *Black Panther,* making history as the first African American to win in the category. Inspired by African tribal wear, Carter fuses traditional and contemporary styles while incorporating technology to deliver fashion and function, cementing her as one of the preeminent voices and experts on Afro aesthetics. With a career spanning more than three decades in theater, cinema, and television, Carter has earned over forty film credits and collaborated with some of the most prolific directors, including Spike Lee, Steven Spielberg, the late John Singleton, Ava DuVernay, and Ryan Coogler. Her outstanding costume design work has been honored with two Academy Award nominations, for *Malcolm X* (1993) and *Amistad* (1998), an Emmy nomination for the reboot of the miniseries *Roots* (2016), the Costume Designers Guild's Career Achievement Award (2019), and a star on the Hollywood Walk of Fame (2021).

HANNAH GIORGIS is a staff writer at *The Atlantic.* Her essays, criticism, and reporting have appeared in publications including *The New York Times Magazine, The Guardian, Bon Appétit,* and *Pitchfork,* as well as at The Ringer and BuzzFeed News, where she worked prior to joining *The Atlantic* in 2018. Most recently she co-wrote *Ida B. The Queen: The Extraordinary Life and Legacy of Ida B. Wells* with Wells's great-granddaughter Michelle Duster, and edited the inaugural collection of essays for Shea Serrano's Halfway Books project, about rap albums including Lil' Kim's *Hard Core,* Kendrick Lamar's *To Pimp a Butterfly,* and The Notorious B.I.G.'s *Life After Death.*

YONA HARVEY is the author of two poetry collections, *You Don't Have to Go to Mars for Love,* winner of the *Believer* Book Award for Poetry, and *Hemming the Water,* winner of the Kate Tufts Discovery Award. She contributed to Marvel's *World of Wakanda,* a companion series to the bestselling *Black Panther* comic, and co-wrote Marvel's *Black Panther and the Crew.*

TRE JOHNSON is a race, culture, and politics writer whose work has appeared in *Rolling Stone,* Vox, *The New York Times, Slate, Vanity Fair,* The Grio, and other outlets. He's provided media commentary via appearances on *CNN Tonight with Don Lemon, CBS Mornings, PBS NewsHour,* NPR's *Morning Edition,* and various podcasts. A 2019 Jack Jones "Culture, Too" Writing Fellow, his first book, the nonfiction historical culture project *Black Genius: Our Celebrations and Our Destructions,* will be published by Dutton Books.

ARVELL JONES is an entrepreneur, graphic artist, and the recipient of Comic-Con International's Ink Pot Award for Lifetime Achievement in recognition of his contribution to television, animation, and comics. His work has appeared in both Marvel and DC Comics from the 1970s through the 1990s, and his art was featured in titles such as *Avengers, Captain America, Thor,* and *Iron Man.* Along with working on movie posters for the Marvel Studios' *Black Panther,* Arvell was recently named one of Marvel's Greatest Creators for Mercedes "Misty" Knight, the first Black female super hero.

FREDERICK JOSEPH is the *New York Times* bestselling author of *The Black Friend, Patriarchy Blues: Reflections on Manhood,* and *Better Than We Found It* (with Porsche Joseph). An award-winning activist, philanthropist, and marketing professional, he was named to the 2019 *Forbes* 30 Under 30 list, is a recipient of the Bob Clampett Humanitarian Award, and was selected for the 2018 Root 100, an annual list of the most influential African Americans. Frederick Joseph lives in New York City with his wife, Porsche, and their dog, Stokely.

SUYI DAVIES OKUNGBOWA is a Nigerian author of fantasy, science fiction, and general speculative fiction and an assistant professor of creative writing at the University of Ottawa, the city where he lives. He has published various novels for adults, the latest of which is *Son of the Storm* (Orbit, 2021), first in the epic fantasy trilogy The Nameless Republic (the second book in the series, *Warrior of the Wind,* is forthcoming). His debut novel, *David Mogo, Godhunter* (Abaddon, 2019) won the 2020 Nommo Award for Best Speculative Novel by an African. His shorter works appear in various periodicals and anthologies, including

Black Panther: Tales of Wakanda, and have been nominated for various awards.

DWAYNE WONG OMOWALE is a Pan-African activist and author who has published several books on the history and culture of Africans and African descendants around the world.

GIL ROBERTSON IV is a veteran lifestyle journalist and film critic. He is also the founder and CEO of the African American Film Critics Association (AAFCA), which represents the largest group of Black film critics in the world.

NIC STONE is the #1 *New York Times* bestselling author of *Dear Martin,* a novel that encourages readers of all ages to have honest discussions about race in today's world. Nic's mission is to create windows through which young people are introduced to new perspectives, and mirrors in which children see their experiences and identities fully represented. All of her novels have been widely embraced by teens and adults and have been the recipients of numerous accolades, awards, and starred reviews. In addition to *Dear Martin,* her books include *Dear Justyce, Blackout,* and the middle-grade novel *Clean Getaway,* all *New York Times* bestsellers, *Odd One Out, Jackpot,* the Shuri series, as well as *Fast Pitch.* A Spelman College graduate, Nic lives in Atlanta with her family. Find her online at nicstone.info or @nicstone.

ABOUT THE ILLUSTRATOR

MATEUS MANHANINI is an illustrator from Brazil, currently based in Rio de Janeiro, who specializes in card-game illustrations, book covers, posters, character designs, and general digital illustrations. He creates bold, edgy illustrations and graphic art for a variety of commercial and personal means that allow imaginative fantasies to turn into vibrant and textured realities. He is best known for his ongoing cover work for clients including Marvel Comics, DC Comics, and BOOM! Studios. He has also collaborated with Penguin Random House, HASBRO/Wizards of the Coast, Universo Guará, and Strange Horizons. Manhanini is a powerful creative force in the workplace and uses his energy for creative problem-solving and to provide high-quality illustrations and unique visuals to his clients. In his free time, Manhanini likes to analyze and capture all the colors of life, and get inspiration from films, especially horror movies.